Thinking Outside the Money Box

The Best Concepts for a Worry-Free Retirement Are Off the Beaten Path

By Mark R. Lumia
CFP®, RMA^SM, ChFC®, CASL®

About *Thinking Outside the Money Box*

"Mark Lumia provides a much-needed retirement security blanket in this book. He shows you how to avoid bumps in the road ahead by planning with useful 'What if' scenarios and examples. You'll also find a wealth of smart retirement income strategies to increase cash flow by optimizing your Social Security and retirement benefits, while minimizing taxes. The result is more income, less tax liability, less investment risk and most important, less worry about retirement."

–Ed Slott, CPA
Retirement expert,
Founder of www.irahelp.com
and www.theslottreport.com

"Thinking Outside the Money Box will help baby boomers make a critical shift in the way they think about money. As boomers move from the accumulation phase of retirement planning to the distribution phase, they will face many issues they've never had to face before: how to maximize Social Security benefits, how to shelter retirement income from taxes, and that all-important question of how not to run out of money. Mark Lumia explains, through solid research and plenty of numbers, how boomers can navigate this new landscape and avoid making mistakes before it's too late."

–Elaine Floyd, CFP®
Director of Retirement and
Life Planning, Horsesmouth, LLC

"Mark joins an illustrious group of RMA[SM] graduates who have written valuable books on retirement planning. In his book, he also refers to a paper published by fellow RMAs[SM] (Sean Ciemiewicz and Christine Russell) in the Retirement Management Journal (RMJ). Mark's additional insights, based on the paper, advance our collective understanding. I was particularly interested in his focus and clear explanations on the various types of annuities.

This is another valuable book written by a fellow RMA[SM] and I am pleased to write this recommendation."

–Francois Gadenne
Chairman of the Board and Executive Director
Retirement Income Industry Association

This publication is designed to provide accurate and authoritative information in regard to the subject matter covered. It is sold with the understanding that the author and publisher are not engaged in rendering legal, investment, tax, insurance, accounting, financial or other professional advice or services. If the reader requires specific advice or services, a competent professional should be consulted at the discretion of the reader.

First Edition

Copyright © 2014 by Mark R. Lumia

Acknowledgments

As I finished this book, I began compiling a list of people I wanted to express my gratitude to, and my first thoughts were of my mother, Margaret Lumia. Mom provided a fine home for me and my two

sisters and worked tirelessly to see to it that we were always well cared for in every way. She knows I love her, but I would like to take this opportunity to say it out loud.

A project such as this just doesn't happen without the support of many people, all of whom gave selflessly of their time, wisdom and energy. I would like to thank my wife, Maryna, whose patience with me and our children is appreciated more than she will ever know. I apologize to her for the blank stares she sometimes received when we were talking and my mind was off somewhere in the pages of this book. (I promise to make it up to you.)

I could never have finished without the able assistance of my administrative team at True Wealth Group, LLC. I also acknowledge the help that my father, Richard Lumia, kindly gave with some of the research that went into this project. Thank you, Dad. I will be forever grateful.

I would be remiss if I didn't make mention of the work of R. Nelson Nash, whose book, *Becoming Your Own Banker – The Infinite Banking Concept,*® provided us with great insight . Also, my thanks to Donald L. Blanton, founder of the Circle of Wealth® System and author of *The Private Reserve Strategy*^TM, from whose knowledge of personal financial management I have greatly benefited. I must include Ed Slott and his organization, Ed Slott's Elite IRA Advisors, for the advanced knowledge I've learned by becoming a Master Elite IRA Advisor. Next is Elaine Floyd, whose system, *Savvy Social Security for Boomers,* inspired me to write articles that were later published in Ed Slott's IRA Advisor newsletter in August 2011 and September 2013.

Conversations throughout the past two decades of my professional life helped forge the direction this book has taken. Most of these conversations happened at events like Peak Advisors Alliance Excell meetings, Money Trax Circle of Wealth® trainings, Master Elite IRA Advisory Group Workshops, Infinite Banking Concepts® Practitioners Think Tank Symposium, and the Retirement Income Industry Association Conference and trainings.

I've been fortunate indeed to have the able assistance of Tina Mailhiot, who helped me proofread the galleys of this publication. Next, my first employee of True Wealth Group, LLC, who has helped me make the company what it is today, Terry LaVergne. And last, but certainly not least, I would like to thank my copy editor, Tom Bowen, for his talent and expertise, as well as the entire creative department at Advisors Excel for their invaluable assistance in getting this information into printed form.

Dedication

This book is dedicated to Maryna, my wife, and my three children, Ian, Mia, and Liam, for showing me the true meaning of life. True Wealth is not about

money. It's about your family and the great relationships you build throughout your life.

Table of Contents

Preface

In South Florida where I grew up, we had a saying: "If you don't like the weather, just stick around a few more minutes – it'll change." Ft. Lauderdale summers were hot and humid. By late afternoon, this heat and humidity would build to a point where something had to give. One minute the sky would be robin's egg blue and cloudless. Then suddenly, seemingly out of nowhere, a dark cloud would block out the sun. The sky would boom and crash with thunder and lightning, and the ensuing downpour would make you run for shelter. A few minutes later, however, the rain would stop as suddenly as it had begun, the crashing and booming would end, and the sun would reappear. Welcome to semi-tropical weather.

Visitors from the north (where else would they be from?) are sometimes alarmed at this sudden weather change. "Hey, the brochure said this was the 'Sunshine State.'" The sun's quick reappearance, however, settles the matter and removes any doubt as to the validity of the state's nickname. We Florida natives, however, have grown to expect violent summertime weather as a part of life and just prepare for it.

I have come to the conclusion that dealing with the uncertainties of life, particularly economic life, is a lot like dealing with the uncertainties of the weather. The more you know and understand, the better you can prepare. The more prepared you are, the less negative impact you will feel.

Nowadays, most of my work as a financial advisor has to do with education and re-education. I say "re-education" because times are changing economically. In the 21st century, the great American dream has morphed from one of hitching our wagon to an ever-ascending star of continual prosperity, high spending, easy credit and soaring debt, to a vision closer to fiscal reality. Many who, during the housing bubble of the early 2000s, obtained two and three mortgages to buy homes they couldn't afford saw their great American dream of home ownership turn into a nightmare. The state in which I live was one of those hit the hardest when the housing bubble burst. Even in the more stable areas of north central Florida, where I now live and work, it was not uncommon as the 2010 decade began to drive through new neighborhoods and see foreclosure signs in front of every other house.

Many in the mid-1990s were accustomed to a stock market that knew only one direction – up. It was as if the entire nation was playing Monopoly, and we all owned Boardwalk. Put down your money on anything that ended in "dot com," and sit back and watch the profits roll in. Storm clouds began forming as the decade advanced, but few paid attention. Even experts on television, whose wisdom we now question, missed all the signs and predicted the Wall Street bull stampede would continue unabated. That's not what happened, of course.

My career in the financial services profession, which began in 1989, has seen the rise and fall of many fortunes. Many who lost as much as half of their life savings to the 2000 stock market crash failed to learn from the experience and suffered what amounted to a knock-out blow in the 2008 crash. There have been many attributions to, and variations of, the wording of the old saying: "Those who do not learn from the past are doomed to repeat it," but the truth of that axiom is undeniable. The 2000 market crash should have taught us a lesson or two about market risk and prudent investing. The fact is, few learned it.

One couple who came to my Fort Lauderdale office, shortly after the 2000 market free fall wiped out nearly 40% of their retirement savings, told me they simply weren't paying attention to what was happening with their money. They had trusted others to manage their money for them, and they had made the mistake of putting too much confidence in their abilities.

"I'm a nurse and he's a landscaper," she said, pointing to her husband. "We don't have time to study what's happening on Wall Street," she continued with moist eyes. "Why didn't anyone tell us this was coming? We could have moved our money somewhere safe."

The question was naïve, but I didn't tell her I thought so. Truth is, no one saw it coming. No one, regardless of how much investing experience they have, or how many letters of the alphabet follow their name, can predict what a market will do, especially the stock market. Yet seeing things through that woman's eyes, the question didn't seem at all naïve. I understood perfectly well how she felt. She felt betrayed. Let's say, for example, that someone planning to purchase a home hired a professional contractor to thoroughly examine the structure before any papers were signed. And let's say this professional contractor told the home buyers that everything was fine. Then, after having lived in the house for a couple of months, suppose the new owners discover that not only is the home poorly constructed, but it is also infested with termites! From my way of looking at it, as Desi said to Lucy with a supercilious look, "Someone has got some explaining to do."

It is the job of professional financial advisors to advise and make recommendations regarding client finances. This is a huge responsibility. True, the broker who advised the nurse and landscaper may not have known that the market would crash. But any competent financial advisor should know enough about the behavior of the stock market in general to have known that what goes up will inevitably come down, and that the closer folks are to retirement, the more of their assets they should have in safe investments and the less money they should have at risk. In the case of this couple, they were both in their late 50s and had never been told to be more conservative with their investments as they approached retirement. Their savings, most of which was in market-based investments, mutual funds and her 401(k), was 100% at risk.

The responses they heard from those into whose hands they had entrusted their financial future all had the same ring to them. "You're not alone: everybody lost money in this one," and "Just stay put, it will come back...eventually." Those responses are accurate on both counts.

Problem is, this couple didn't have "eventually" to wait. They were left deciding how much longer they would have to postpone their retirement to allow them time to rebuild their savings.

Because I choose to specialize in safe-money investing, very few of my clients lost money during those two financial disasters – at least not in the accounts over which I had oversight. While I did not mention this to the couple, I must confess to a surge of satisfaction and pride at that thought. The task ahead of me with this pair, I knew, was to help them pick up the pieces and begin again. I knew we must find them a strategy that would enable them to regain as much of their losses as possible, and this time around, build a financial house that would never again be threatened by the stormy skies of a turbulent stock market.

During my college days at the University of Florida, I eschewed reading as if it were a contagious disease. But for some reason, after I left college and entered the business world, I began devouring books of every type. In one book about human psychology, the author posed this question: "If something you thought was true turned out to be false, when would you want to know it?" Right away, I said to myself, and meant it. But the sad truth related in the book was that many close their minds to ideas that are contrary to their own pre-conceived notions. How sad is that?

If I'm driving on a road that has a bridge out up ahead, I'm very interested in knowing that little piece of information. While I normally have a disdain for those ubiquitous orange traffic barrels I see so many of here in Florida, I would be grateful for them if they warned me of an impending disaster. Likewise, if my assets were improperly placed, or invested in such a way that my financial future was at risk, I would want to know that information as soon as possible.

Many of the concepts and ideas we will discuss in the pages of this book may challenge what you have always thought to be true. I invite you to engage those concepts and ideas with an open mind and resist the tendency to cling to traditional views out of sheer habit. It is a time to know the truth about money, investing, retirement, and wealth preservation and taxes, and stand in that truth for the benefit of ourselves, our families and our heirs. The views expressed here will be not only mine, but those of many whose research has paved the way. More than that, the points made in the next few chapters will make logical sense to you. Of that I'm certain.

Chapter One

Why Seek Financial Advice
From a Specialist?

I f you needed heart surgery tomorrow, would you go to your primary care physician for the operation? I doubt it. If you're going to have your heart worked on, you want a specialist – someone who has spent a few years studying nothing but the circulatory system and who knows his way around the chest cavity. Do you concur? I assure you I am by no means casting aspersions on general practitioners or the role they play in keeping us healthy. As a matter of fact, a general practitioner is trained to know a little bit about everything that goes on with our bodies. You could even say that these doctors *specialize* in *generality* when it comes to the practice of medicine. They are on the front lines, so to speak. They are the first ones to spot it when something isn't quite right. As you would expect, when they detect some ailment beyond their scope of expertise, they will not hesitate to refer you to a specialist for further treatment. It should work that way in the financial profession, but, unfortunately it usually doesn't. There are many generalists in the financial advisory field who, for whatever reason, don't always refer their clients to specialists when they should. Take retirement income planning, for example, the area in which I specialize. It is as intricate and delicate to your wealth as brain surgery could be to your health, as this and subsequent chapters of this book will show.

The story is told about an old man who was a mechanic. Because he lived near a seaport, he became especially acquainted with the kind of large diesel engines that power ocean-going vessels. The man had all the work he wanted and he would have retired years earlier, but he enjoyed what he was doing and was highly sought after for his skills.

A cruise ship limped into port one morning experiencing engine trouble. The owners of the ocean liner, unaware of the old mechanic or his skills, had arranged for their own expert mechanics to be flown in by helicopter to repair the enormous engine. But they were unable to figure out the problem. Another crew was flown in to repair the engine but they also failed. Finally, someone told the owners about the old man and so they called him out of desperation, although they doubted he could help.

When he showed up at the dock, there was nothing in the old man's appearance that made them think otherwise. He was shabbily dressed and a bit stooped with age. Saying little, the old man withdrew a hammer from his tool bag and set about listening to the idling engine, pausing here and there to study the workings of the giant motor. After about an hour of this, one of the engineers, wishing to know what the old man was listening for, began to speak. The old man held up a bony index finger, requesting silence. A few minutes later the old man went over to a large flywheel and gave it one solid lick with his ball peen hammer. The flywheel began to move. Listening a few minutes more for sounds that only he could understand, the old man nodded, satisfied that the engine was in good working order, replaced the hammer in his tool bag, and left the ship.

A week later, the owners of the ship received a bill from the old man for $5,000. They were shocked.

"But he was only here an hour, and all he did was tap the engine with a hammer," protested one of the owners.

"Send the bill back and tell him to give us an itemized statement," said the other owner.

The old man complied with the request, submitting a second bill which read:

Tapping with hammer -	$100
Knowing where to tap with hammer -	$4,900

The old man knew, and he knew that he knew. He didn't need to consult books and diagrams, pore over pages from the manufacturer's operations manual, ask consultants or seek solutions from some outside source. He had experience and he possessed a unique understanding of his craft that was the product of years of learning the nuances of his trade and filing away those findings until he needed to retrieve them. That's what makes a specialist. They focus their knowledge like a laser beam and apply it to the problem at hand.

Ed Slott is a specialist in the field of Individual Retirement Accounts. He has written several books on the subject, including *Stay Rich for Life* and *The Retirement Savings Time Bomb...and How to Diffuse It*, and has become a national television celebrity because of his expertise in this one subject. He knows IRAs and 401(k)s the way a skilled carpenter knows wood. With 10,000 baby boomers retiring every day, Slott's expertise couldn't have come along at a better time.

According to data collected by the Investment Company Institute, retirement savings accounted for 36% of all household financial assets in the United States in 2012 with the bulk of that money, around $9 trillion, sitting in IRAs and defined contribution plans, such as 401(k)s. Most people approaching retirement know about as much about the actual workings of these financial instruments as they do about the plumbing inside the walls of their homes. With so many Americans approaching retirement, the time has come to make some decisions about what to do with those accounts, and knowledge about the inner workings of tax-deferred savings plans is more and more in demand.

I have the privilege of serving as a member of Ed Slott's Master Elite IRA Advisor Group, an elite corps of financial advisors specially trained in the kind of retirement planning that involves qualified accounts, such as IRAs and 401(k)s. To use a military analogy, they are to retirement planning what Navy Seals are to rescue missions. When I was asked in 2011 to submit a guest article for Ed Slott's monthly newsletter, I didn't realize what an honor it was until I learned that he only publishes guest articles three or four times a year. The article I submitted was entitled "Coordinating Social Security with IRAs." I chose that topic because (a) it is an area in which I have received much training and acquired much experience, and (b) I am passionate about keeping this part of retirement mistake-free. Asking me to give you my opinions about this area of retirement planning is like asking Smoky the Bear to give a talk on fire prevention. I have a lot to say. Why? Because making prudent choices in this area can mean thousands of additional dollars in retirement, and because this turf can be treacherous if you don't know what you're doing; you need a good guide – someone who has a "map to the minefield," so to speak.

The big decision is when to take your Social Security when you have an IRA. An associate of mine here in the Lady Lake, Florida, office likes to call it "pulling the trigger" on Social Security income. You have the option to begin your Social Security payments as early as age 62, wait until you are age 66, or delay taking Social Security until age 70. I was quoted in the April 2012 issue of *Financial Planning* magazine as urging retirees not to make an impulsive decision regarding this and to please see a specialist about retirement planning before making a decision.

A client came into the office one afternoon faced with a choice. She was 66 years old and was still working as a professor at a local university. She loved her work and didn't plan on retiring until she turned 70. The woman had attended one of my workshops and filled out a one-page pre-appointment form. The form is akin to the kind you fill out in the doctor's office, letting the doctor know details regarding your medical history and what medication you may be taking. The doctor needs this kind of information in order to effectively treat or examine you. How can she fix you if she doesn't know what's broken?

It's the same way with financial planning. The questionnaire asks the basic questions you would expect before a financial planning appointment. On the day of the appointment, I was looking over the form and I noticed this woman had filled every section but the one having to do with her marital status. I decided it was perhaps a touchy subject, and that I would approach it gingerly in my initial interview. For obvious reasons, marital status is basic information a financial planner needs in order to effectively help a client. But it is on the personal side. I decided I would approach it gingerly in case it was a delicate topic. But there was no real reason for my caution. The woman had inadvertently skipped over that section of the form. As it turned out, she didn't mind sharing the information at all. She told me she was a widow, and that her husband had died in 2000 after 33 years of marriage. Upon hearing that, I asked her if she knew that she was entitled to survivor benefits.

The woman related how she made a personal visit to the local Social Security office where she was told that she was not eligible for her husband's survivor benefit, but the reason wasn't explained to her. She was ineligible merely because she was only 54 at the time. At 60 she could have received 71.5% of his survivor benefit.

It has been my experience with professionals, especially educators, that they sometimes become so wrapped up in their work that it's hard for them to focus on such mundane things as what they are entitled to in the way of Social Security benefits after a spouse dies. She apologized for "not knowing how those things worked." I told her that it was quite all right because it gave people like me a job to do.

In the professor's case, it turned out to be one of those "all's well that ends well" situations. Had she taken her survivor benefits as soon as she was eligible for them, she would have only received 71.5% of the full amount. Because she waited until age 66 to take them, she stands to receive the full amount. It's that way with Social Security benefits. Uncle Sam makes a deal with you. Go ahead and take the money now and receive 28.5% less, or wait until you are age 66 and receive the full amount. I'm sure they have actuaries on staff who can accurately predict what percentage of people are eligible for benefits, but choose to wait until they can receive the full amount...and then die while waiting.

My knowledge of how the movement of stars and planets affects our lives is limited to the lyrics of the rock musical *Hair,* and an occasional glimpse at the horoscope in the Sunday newspaper. But in the professor's case it was as if all the planets and stars were perfectly aligned for her in this respect. She wasn't aware of her benefits to begin with, and by waiting she was able to receive more than she otherwise would have. She was entitled to receive $2,131 every month for the next four years. That's a total of $102,288 that she may have passed up. Needless to say, she was excited to have discovered what she considered to be a windfall but was actually money hiding in plain sight. She told me it was comforting for her to know that now she could retire if she wanted to. We discussed when she should take her Social Security. She was also not aware of the fact that if she waited until she was age 70 to begin taking her Social Security benefits, her payout would increase by 32% - considerably more!

Do I want vanilla or chocolate? Either way, you're still getting ice cream.

"Nice to have such decisions to make," she said.

She decided to continue working until age 70. I don't blame her. Had she been miserable in her job, she may have made a different decision. We figured it up. By earning the delayed credits and COLAs between the ages of 70 and 88, she will have collected $200,000 more, in addition to her survivor benefit, by waiting.

Thinking Outside the Box

"Think outside the box" is one of those catchphrases that gain traction (oops, there's another one) in the workplace of professionals. Others are "bottom line" (an old one) and "at the end of the day" (a more recent cliché). "Think outside the box" came along in the 1970s and means to think creatively, unimpeded by orthodox or conventional constraints. The obvious implication is that the "box" is square and rigid, thus an apt symbol for unimaginative thinking. By contrast, to have ideas that are outside the "box" is to remove the mental fetters that bind us to traditional patterns and to engage in (here's another one) "blue sky" thinking. Pushing the limits of our creativity enables us to see solutions we might not otherwise catch sight of.

I am continually amazed at how so many traditional planners are unwilling to do this. Personally, I scan the retirement products daily and peruse the media on a regular basis looking for solutions. The professional financial planning landscape is ever changing, just like the economic environment. The financial advisor who comes to work and has a tool box that contains only three or four options for his clients cannot serve them well. Those advisors, even if they do "think outside the box," remain shackled if they can only represent one company or one financial planning concept.

I think it was Sam Loyd who first came up with the puzzle known as the "Nine Dots Puzzle," which illustrates the concept of unconventional thinking. In his 1914 book, *Sam Loyd's Cyclopedia of 5000 Puzzles, Tricks, and Conundrums (With Answers),* there appeared nine dots similar to the ones below. The challenge is to connect the dots using four straight strokes of the pen without lifting it from the paper.

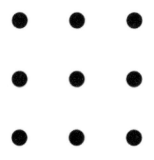

Stumped? Most folks who aren't familiar with the puzzle try to draw their lines without extending them beyond the "walls" suggested by the placement of the dots. But the challenge said nothing about whether the lines could go (drum roll, please) ***outside the box!***

Solved, the puzzle looks like this:

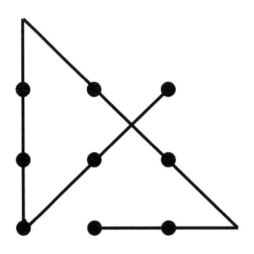

In retirement planning the "puzzle," more often than not, is finding a way to help a client retire when they have finite resources and a specific income need. Example: "We have our Social Security of $2,300 per month, no pension, a paid-for house, and a 401(k) worth $200,000. We owe $15,000 in consumer debt and have no long-term care insurance. When can we retire?"

Thinking outside the box is the antithesis of trying to hammer a square solution peg into a round planning hole. If an advisor is a captive representative of a large brokerage house with only limited concepts and products at his or her disposal, they wind up having to do just that most of the time. I believe that proper planning – planning where the solution matches the problem, calls for a holistic approach. Once you understand how holistic problem solving works, you wonder how anyone could operate a financial planning practice without it.

The Best Specialists Are Holistic Specialists

A 70-year-old man who owned his own repair business came into the office one morning for a consultation but said there was probably little we could do to help him because he had no real retirement savings, only $30,000 he had socked away. But I believe in doing what one can with what one has, so our interview proceeded. As I looked at the man's earnings statements over the previous ten years, I noticed something puzzling. For the last seven years prior to his walking into my office, he had earned between $9,000 and $14,600 per year. Immediately prior to that, however, his income was in the $60,000 range, and had been for approximately 20 years. He explained that eight years or so ago, he went to an accountant who suggested that he set up a Limited Liability Corporation (LLC). The accountant also suggested that he claim between $9,000 and $14,600 as income, and receive the rest as dividends.

The accountant meant well. He was trying to reduce the man's taxes. But the accountant had failed to realize that Social Security income is based on the highest 35 years of one's income. Those seven years where the man's income was adjusted artificially lower may have saved him some in taxes, but it would also negatively affect how much he would receive in Social Security benefits when he retired and for the rest of his life.

This is a perfect example of how solving one problem can, if you aren't careful, create another. I recommend that when seeking professional financial help of any kind that you try to obtain the services of someone who can look at the entire picture and make holistic recommendations. Just as holistic medicine involves treating the whole body with a remedy that acknowledges the interdependence of each of the body's individual parts, a holistic financial advisor will take into account the entire financial landscape so as not to create one problem while solving another.

I am reminded of the children's song entitled: "There Was an Old Woman Who Swallowed a Fly." The lyrics tell the absurd tale of a woman who swallowed increasingly larger animals to swallow the one she had just ingested, until she finally dies. I always thought it was rather dark humor for children, but the humor behind the lyrics lies in the idea that the woman clearly should have died after swallowing the bird, which she swallowed to swallow the fly. But the old woman miraculously endures swallowing several quadrupeds, such as cows and even a horse, before the bizarre behavior comes to a fateful end.

Solving one problem and causing another is sometimes seen in nature, where we hear about well-meaning but misguided scientists introducing one species to curb the growth of another species. Up until 1935, Australia had no native toads. But in that year they began importing toads to eat the beetles that were damaging sugar cane crops. Before long, the toads were out of control. They were multiplying so fast that they entered the natural habitats of Australia's rare freshwater crocodiles. The crocs didn't know that the cane toad's skin was lethally poisonous. According to *The Guardian,* a Sydney, Australia, newspaper, the population of the rare freshwater crocodile was soon decimated as a result.

A holistic financial planner is able to see the entire picture and is trained to understand how one piece of the financial puzzle connects with another. In football, for example, the quarterback and the offensive lineman are both football players, but by the very nature of the positions they play, they approach the game much differently. The quarterback's job is more holistic in nature. He must pay attention to the entire field and makes decisions based on what the defense is doing thirty and forty yards away, while the lineman's job is limited in scope to what's right in front of him. He isn't supposed to see the play developing forty yards away. His job is to block the defensive lineman who is looking him in the eye. By the very definition of his role on the field, his field of vision will be of necessity a limited one.

Unfortunately some financial professionals, because they lack the training to "see the entire field" will advise clients from their limited field of vision. There's an old expression that has various attributions and wording, but the thought is valid: "When all you have is a hammer, everything looks like a nail." If an accountant, for example, is merely focusing on lowering taxes, he may advise a client to make a move that will indeed lower taxes, as was in the case of the man who formed an LLC to reduce his reportable earnings, but will cause the forfeiture of some other advantage in another area of his financial landscape.

The Value of "What-If" Tax Returns

A specialist will know where to look to find things a generalist won't know to look for. About a year ago at the time of this writing, a woman came into our office for a financial checkup. In reviewing her taxes, we found something interesting. We are CFPs® (Certified Financial Planners®) and not CPAs (Certified Public Accountants), but as CFPs® we do have some training on taxes and how they interact with other aspects of the entire financial picture. As a matter of fact, we often work with CPAs, especially the ones who wish to help the client holistically and not just fill out a tax return.

The woman had $300,000 in a traditional IRA. On line 60 of her tax return, she was paying zero taxes, but because her money was in a traditional IRA, that would soon change. According to Internal Revenue Service regulations, when you have your money in an IRA, you pay no taxes on the gains until you reach 70½. Then on April 1 the year after the year you turn 70½, you must start taking Required Minimum Distributions, whether you need the money or not, and pay the IRS its fair share of the tax on the money withdrawn. The amount you must take is predicated on IRS life expectancy tables. The woman said she had seen the same CPA and the same financial advisor for the past 10 years.

"Have they recommended that you do a 'what-if' return?" I asked her. She said no.

The purpose of a "what-if" return is to see if there is a way to re-position money in such a way as to enhance either the tax picture or the income picture or both.

In the "what-if" return that we did, I was able to show her how she could move $16,250 from her traditional IRA to a Roth IRA. With a Roth IRA, there are no RMDs. For the last 10 years, if someone had only advised her, she could have been removing $16,250 every year, for the last 10 years, and putting it into a Roth IRA. It would've cost her zero dollars to move the money every year. The Roth would continue to grow tax-deferred, and she could get it out tax-free with no RMDs.

On top of that, we did a second "what-if" return. She could have also done an extra $14,000 and this time in a 10% bracket that $14,000 would've cost her $1,400 in taxes. So what does all of that total? $16,250 + $14,000 = $30,250. In 10 years she could have moved the entire $300,000 and it would have cost her $14,000 to do that – $1,400 each year for those 10 years. So for the cost of only $14,000 all of her money could have been inside a Roth IRA, which would have enabled her to have her money growing tax-deferred and tax-free upon withdrawal, with no RMDs.

Needless to say the woman was very upset that no one had pointed out these strategies to her before, and I don't blame her. Those were things that one would not expect her to know. But you would expect that knowledge to be possessed by someone who chose to give financial advice as a profession.

Like everyone else, I expect my experts to know what they are doing. When I go to the doctor, I expect good science and a straight answer, even if it's not what I want to hear. When I take my automobile in for service, I expect it to receive the proper adjustments from technicians with adequate training and proper tools. I expect them to understand my make and model of automobile. I expect the shop to own the proper equipment that will diagnose mechanical problems and set my automobile in good working order. When I fly, I don't really care so much what in-flight movie is playing, but I do expect the pilots to be sober and know the meaning of every dial and switch in the cockpit. I also expect them to possess the skill to take off and land without incident. Is that asking too much? No. It is not asking too much of any paid professional to know his or her business.

There is no one-size-fits-all in the world of financial planning. Every case is different. In the decades during which I have been involved in financial planning, I have seen many scenarios and it has been my observation that no two are identical. This is altogether appropriate. No two people are exactly alike. No, not even identical twins. And just when you think you can't be surprised, you will be.

You Won the What?

Not too long ago, a couple who had made an appointment came in with a healthy stack of statements and documents for me to review, including the last three years' tax returns. I usually only ask for the last two years' tax returns, but they explained that there was a special reason why they needed to bring the one from three years ago. It seems that was the year they won the lottery. The husband had put down a dollar into a group ticket, thinking nothing would ever come of it. But when the numbers were called, the seven people who wrote their names on the ticket had won $16 million. These lucky seven had already agreed to share any winnings equally among themselves. By taking the lump sum and paying taxes, their cut was approximately $1.4 million each.

I noticed that the couple's earnings for the previous year were zero. I suppose winning the lottery can have that effect on you. His interest and income dividends totaled $1,000, so that was his adjusted gross income for the year. They had the standard deductions, and two exemptions, which, when totaled up, amounted to $19,000. Line 43 on his 1040 (taxable income) appropriately read "zero." But I explained that because he wasn't using the $18,000 in deductions and exemptions, it was as if he were just wasting $18,000. I showed him where he could move $18,000 from a traditional IRA, where a good chunk of his money sat, over to a Roth IRA and it would cost nothing. When the picture became clear, I saw a big grin form on his face.

But taking it a step further, he can move $83,000 from the traditional IRA to the Roth, and it would only cost him around $10,000 to do it. If he were to do that over the next several years before he turns 70, then he is going to be able to move his traditional IRA into a Roth IRA and at age 70 his Social Security is going to be nearly doubled because of the Cost of Living Adjustments and the delayed credits. So we could increase his income and reduce taxes at the same time. Both their smiles couldn't have been bigger.

As opposed to generalists, specialists are able to spot movements such as this because they are constantly updating their fund of knowledge with reports such as the NBER report discussed here, reports from the University of Pennsylania's Wharton School, one of the most respected business schools in the country, and reports from the federal government, such as the U.S. General Accounting Office report. Keeping up to date on all that is current in the financial field is necessary in order to maintain such designations and titles as Certified Financial Planner®, Retirement Management Analyst^{SM}, Master Elite IRA Advisor, Chartered Financial Consultant®, Certified Advisor for Senior Living®, Circle of Wealth Master Mentor and Infinite Banking Practitioner®.

A June 2011 GAO report, for example, contained information vital for anyone entering retirement. The heading of the report read: "RETIREMENT INCOME – Ensuring Income throughout Retirement Requires Difficult Choices." In this government report, the admonition was clearly spelled out that it is wise to (a) delay taking your Social Security and (b) to add an annuity to your retirement portfolio to make sure that you do not outlive your income. Just as a surgeon keeps track of medical journals and reports so as to remain competent in his field of expertise, a financial specialist keeps current with reports such as the GAO report mentioned above. If one is to advise clients on matters having to do with their finances, one must keep up with the times.

There Are No Cookie Cutter Solutions

Every time I read a headline that says "78 Million Baby Boomers Set to Retire," I can't help but think of the movie *March of the Penguins* that came out in 2005 and was narrated by Morgan Freeman. Inerasable from my mind is the sight of thousands of Emperor penguins as they march as one huddled, tuxedoed mass across the ice deserts of Antarctica, traversing some of the most inhospitable terrain on Earth, to reach their traditional breeding ground. There's one scene where an endless stream of penguins is shown waddling single file across the ice, guided by instinct, I suppose, to their goal of propagating the penguin species. Each penguin is in lock step, following the movements of the penguin in front without looking up.

That may be just fine for penguins, but when it comes to plotting and charting our course into retirement, we humans will require strategies that match our individual needs. No lock-step march and no cookie-cutter retirement plan can get the job done. There is no one-size-fits-all in this endeavor. Much of what goes into an effective retirement plan will depend on your dreams, goals, objectives, risk tolerance, family life and health. Myths of investing and money management have impeded the progress of many who tend to follow the herd. If you are in the "red zone" of retirement (10 years on either side), it is critical that you keep your focus and play smart.

Chapter Two

Effectively Regulating Your Cash Flow

How you regulate your cash flow can make the difference between financial success and financial failure. Thanks to software developer Don Blanton, we have "The Personal Economic Flow Model" to give us a visual picture of how money flows. If you are able to visualize your money from perhaps a different perspective than you have ever seen it before, it may help you to increase the overall efficiency of how you manage your cash flow.

To begin with, you have a lifetime wealth and income potential. Everyone does. It's the total amount of money that will pass through your hands during your working years. It is a large but finite amount. The primary source of capital is probably the earnings from your occupation. You may also have other sources – an inheritance, for example. We usually receive our money from our employer on a weekly or monthly basis. For some the amount varies up and down from pay period to pay period. For others it is a fixed amount. A portion of it will be lost to income taxes, of course. But imagine that money in a large tank that is being fed by your paychecks week in and week out. At the bottom of the tank is an outflow pipe. Fortunately for you, there is a regulator valve that you can control. You can choose to divert some of your lifetime capital into savings and investments. Imagine two tanks above that valve, one marked "Savings" and one marked "Investments." Money that flows directly into your lifestyle is lost and gone forever. What flows out of the lifestyle pipe is spent and just evaporates.

Blanton says you can ignore the regulator valve if you choose to, living up every penny of what you earn and ending up with nothing when you reach retirement. Or you can adjust the valve, redirecting a calculated amount of money into your retirement savings and investment program so that you will be comfortable in retirement. How much should you save and invest? Good question! Before you can answer that question, you need to know the answer to the following questions posed by Blanton:

1. What return would I have to earn on my savings and investments for my current plan to work?

2. What is the minimum amount of money I need to be putting away each year to enjoy my present lifestyle during retirement?

3. How long would I have to work before I can retire and enjoy my present standard of living until my life expectancy?

4. What is the most I will be able to spend in retirement and have my money last through my life expectancy and beyond?

That little Lifestyle Regulator Valve you control determines how much income you allocate to your lifestyle and how much you wish to pump into your savings and investment tanks. I use the word "pump" because it doesn't happen naturally. It requires effort to save and invest. The tanks into which you divert these are long-term accounts. These two tanks will provide you with the money you need to live on when the inflow of your weekly or monthly paychecks stops. You may also use these tanks to help finance major capital purchases, such as cars, education and weddings during your accumulation years.

Imagine these two tanks into which you divert savings and investments are marked *"Safe"* and *"Risk."* Every dollar deposited into the savings tank is safe. That is, there is no potential for loss unless you move it. The investment tank is marked "Risk" because it potentially offers a higher return but comes with a degree of risk. Money levels in this tank can fluctuate up and down over time. There is also no top on this tank.

It would be prudent to pay attention to how much you put into each tank, Safe and Risk, as you get older. When you are just starting out, perhaps the lion's share of what you set aside should first be in the savings tank until you build up an emergency fund. Then, during your peak earning years, divert more money into the investment, or Risk tank. Then as you grow older, divert more and more into the Safe tank. A good rule of thumb would be to have enough money in your savings tank to cover any major purchase. A major purchase is anything you wish to buy that you can't pay for in full from your monthly cash flow.

Is it possible to withdraw money from these long-term accounts during your accumulation years? Of course! And emergencies sometime arise that may require that. But failure to put it back can be a costly decision down the road. Also, during retirement it is essential to keep an eye on the lifestyle regulator. You don't want to run out of money. You may even wish to pass some of what you have accumulated on to the next generation.

Look at all the things in the category of "lifestyle" that can be a drain on your resources:

- Sales taxes
- Education costs
- Food
- Clothing
- Phone
- Cars
- Gas
- Vacations
- Maintenance

- Medical Insurance
- Property Taxes
- Auto Insurance
- Home Owners Insurance
- Life Insurance
- Weddings
- Cable TV
- Giving . . . and the list goes on.

The Lifestyle Regulator Valve is the most important piece of equipment in this money plumbing system. The more you pay attention to it during the period of time when money is flowing into your Lifetime Capital Potential tank, the better off you will be during your retirement years.

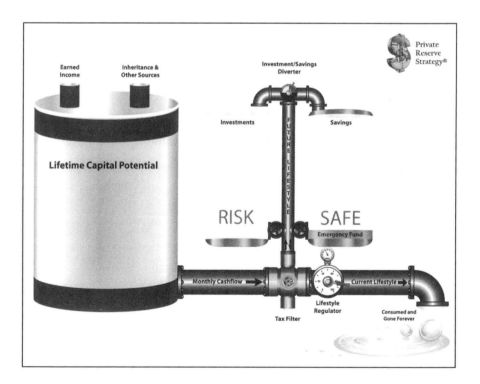

Chapter Three

What Baby Boomers Need to Know about Social Security

To copy a page from the inimitable Jeff Foxworthy, who made his mark on American audiences with "You may be a redneck if..." jokes, you may be a *baby boomer* if:

- You know what a "sock hop" is.
- You ever listened to "The Lone Ranger" on the radio.
- You know who Howdy Doody was.
- You ever used Brylcreem.
- You can complete this song lyric: "I wonder, wonder, wonder, wonder who..."
- The first photos of you are in black and white.
- You ever used a metal ice tray with a lever.
- Your family had one automobile and it had fins.
- You know what a pet rock is.
- Sean Connery will always be James Bond to you.
- Your first allowance was payable to you in change.

Officially, baby boomers are those who were born between the years 1946 and 1964 when the birth rate in America rose dramatically following World War II. Those post-war babies have shaped the country and the world socially, philosophically and economically, and they are still doing it. The earliest of the boom generation are turning 65 at a rate of 10,000 per day. Words they applied to "old people" in the heyday of their own youth, such as "retirement" and "Social Security," are now being used in connection with them.

Phillip Longman, in his research paper entitled, "Why Are So Many Baby Boomers Ill Prepared for Retirement?" makes the point that while boomers were great at inventing rock and roll and landing a man on the moon, the generation that gave us consumer credit and the two-car garage wasn't so good at preparing for their golden years. While boomers earned more at every age of life than any other generation in history, they weren't so good at saving it. The parents of boom children knew all about hard times. They were children of the Great Depression of the 1930s. But boomers were blessed with a cornucopia of plenty. Consumer credit made it easy to obtain new automobiles, nice homes with color televisions in each room and push-button gadgets that would have awed their grandparents.

If you are a baby boomer and can think back to when your parents retired, they probably didn't give Social Security too much thought. They just drove down to their local Social Security office as soon as they turned 65, or maybe at age 62 if they retired early, and applied for benefits. They took their benefits for granted and didn't ask many questions. Boomers, however, are approaching Social Security in a much different way. They have questions. "Will Social Security be there for me? How much can I expect to receive? When should I start taking my Social Security Benefits?"

Will Social Security Be Here for Me?

Baby boomers have all heard the rumor that Social Security is "going broke." Is it true? Many of them may be wondering if they will someday get a letter marked "urgent!" by the Social Security Administration informing them that they would like to sincerely apologize, but this will be their last check because the kitty is out of cash. It's a legitimate concern, all right.

In the 1990s, the financial services industry started sounding the alarm about Social Security in an effort to get baby boomers to save for retirement. Analysts pointed out that when Social Security was first instituted in 1935, there were some 40 workers paying into the system for every one retiree drawing benefits. But when baby boomers would be ready to retire, there would be only two or three workers paying into the system for every retiree drawing benefits. The math didn't look so good.

But, like many things, what started out as a notification alarm bell quickly grew to an "end-of-the-world" red alert. These irrational fears and misunderstandings about the solvency of the Social Security system have, in my opinion, gotten out of hand. Let's look now at what the Social Security trustees say. Every year, they publish a comprehensive report showing the long-range outlook for Social Security, or the Old Age Survivors and Disability Insurance (OASDI) program, the official name for Social Security.

According to the 2011 Social Security Board of Trustees' annual report, OASDI trust funds spent $736 billion in 2011, primarily paying out benefits to approximately 55 million people. Payments went to 38 million retired workers and their dependents, six million survivors of deceased workers and 11 million disabled workers. An estimated 158 million people paid payroll taxes in 2011, contributing $564 billion to the Social Security trust funds. All of that money going into the trust funds doesn't just sit there. It earns interest. In 2011, that interest amounted to $114 billion, an effective annual interest rate of about 4.4%. Not too bad.

Now, granted, the trustees report indicated that trust funds are projected to be exhausted by 2033 unless changes are made. Several reforms were suggested that, over the next 75 years, would restore the program to solvency. But these plans will not be implemented for years to come. Meanwhile the trustees report confirms that Social Security's trust funds are solvent and continue to grow. Even if left unchanged, which is unlikely to happen, the system would have enough to maintain full benefits until 2033.

What types of reforms are suggested? Although the Social Security system is not in imminent danger, most people agree that the earlier reforms are instituted, the less painful they will be on everyone. After all, we want our children and their children after them to benefit as we have. Here are just a few of the ideas that have been proposed:

- Increase the maximum earnings subject to Social Security tax. At this writing, $113,700 in earnings is subject to the 6.2% tax paid by you and your employer.

- Raise the normal retirement age to match life expectancy. As of this writing, full retirement age is 66 for people born between 1943 and 1954, and 67 for people born in 1960 or later.

- Change the benefit formula so that future increases would occur at a slower pace. This would affect the benefits of future retirees.

- Change the formula for cost-of-living adjustments. This could give retirees smaller benefit increases going forward, although the changes are expected to be minimal.

The bottom line for baby boomers is that their Social Security benefits are not likely to be affected much, if at all.

How Much Will I Receive?

Of course you want to know how much you stand to receive when you begin collecting your Social Security. As you will see by reading this book, a lot of that depends on you and the decisions you make in the next few years. One of the functions of a professional retirement planner is that of nailing down the answer to that question. If you don't have that answer nailed down, how can you do a budget and position your assets to adequately care for your expenses and meet your financial retirement goals? It would be like shooting at a moving target. When your Social Security benefit is calculated, it will be based on how much you earned over your working career and at what age you apply for benefits.

The formula for calculating Social Security is pretty complex. You may or may not want to follow along with this. If you don't like the nuts and bolts of things, just skip to the next heading. But if you are like some people, you will find the formula interesting. You can use it to determine your own Social Security benefits.

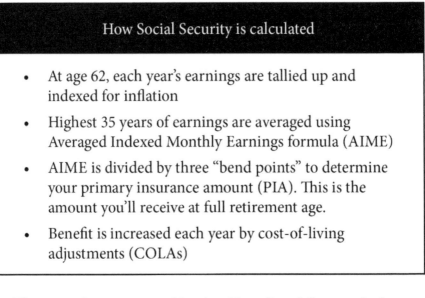

The general process goes like this: First, Social Security looks at your annual earnings over your entire lifetime, indexes them for inflation, and picks the 35 highest years' earnings to include in the formula. The indexed earnings are then totaled and divided by 35 to come up with an average. If you don't have 35 years of earnings, the missing years will be filled in with zeroes. This has the effect of lowering Social Security benefits for parents, for example, who have taken time off work to care for children. However, they may be eligible for spousal benefits (more on that later).

Next, a formula is applied to your average indexed monthly earnings to determine your primary insurance amount. This is the amount you will receive when you reach full retirement age. As mentioned earlier, if you were born between 1943 and 1954, your full retirement age is 66. Each year, annual cost of living adjustments (COLAs) are applied to your benefit to help keep up with inflation.

Want to see an example of how this works? Let's say that Joe B. Boomer, born in 1950, earned the Social Security maximum every year since he was 22. His average indexed monthly earnings would work out to be $8,238. In calculating his primary insurance amount (PIA), the first $767 would be multiplied by 90%. The amount between $767 and $4,624, or $3,857, would then be multiplied by 32%. And the amount over $4,624, or $3,614, would be multiplied by 15%. These amounts would be totaled to come up with a PIA of $2,466.60. This is the amount the worker would receive at full retirement age. I told you it was complicated. But that's the government for you.

Example of benefit formula	
• Baby boomer age born in 1950	
• Maximum Social Security earnings every year since age 22	
• AIME = $8,238	
• PIA formula:	
$767 x .90 =	$690.30
$3,857 x .32 =	1,234.24
$3,614x .15 =	542.10
Total	$2,466.64

What Happens If I Apply for Benefits Early?

There's an entire chapter on this later in the book, and as we go forward, I think you will see just how important the answer to this question is. But for now, remember I said that your primary insurance amount, or PIA, is the benefit you will receive at full retirement age. So what happens if you apply for Social Security before you turn 66? Your benefit will be reduced. You will receive a percentage of your PIA depending on when you apply. If you apply at age 62, you will receive 75% of your PIA, at 63, 80%, and so on. These amounts are prorated, so you can apply anytime between the ages of 62 and 66 and your benefit will be reduced by the appropriate amount. Here's an example: If you were born between 1943 and 1954 and you:

Apply at age	Benefit will be % of PIA	Example if PIA is $2,466
62	75.0%	$1,850
63	80.0%	$1,973
64	86.7%	$2,137
65	93.3%	$2,302
66	100%	$2,466

What Happens if I Apply after Full Retirement Age?

Excellent question! Full attention is also given to this in a subsequent chapter, but for now, the short answer is that if you apply for Social Security after you turn 66, you will earn delayed credits of 8% for each year you delay. So if you apply at 67, your benefit will be 108% of your PIA. At 68 it will be 116%, and so on. After age 70 you can't earn any more delayed credits, so it doesn't pay to wait until after age 70 to apply for Social Security. Here's an example. If you were born between 1943 and 1954 and you:

Apply at age	Benefit will be % of PIA	Example if PIA is $2,466
67	108%	$2,663
68	116%	$2,861
69	124%	$3,058
70	132%	$3,255

Note: COLAs are not factored into these amounts.

Calculating Your Social Security

Hey, Mark! Is there an easier way to find out about how much you can expect to receive in Social Security benefits? Yes, actually, there is. You can dig out your annual Social Security statement, if you still have it. If not, you may go online and get it. To save costs, the Social Security Administration stopped mailing out annual statements. But as part of the Paperwork Reduction Act of 1995, you can probably access your statement online. You will have to jump through some hoops to get it, but the hoops aren't too difficult. Go to this website: secure.ssa.gov/RIL/SiView.do and create an account. After agreeing to the terms of service, which has some comforting words about protecting your identity, and then a stiff-finger warning about providing false information, you can proceed to answer a few questions and set up your account. You may be surprised at how much of your work history Uncle Sam has been keeping up with. Under the "Earnings Record" tab of your "My Social Security" statement you will find your earnings history chronicled from your first job at the local car wash to your last year's tax return. Looking at it in the format in which they present it, it sort of reminds me of the way tree rings reflect the good years and the lean years, income-wise.

On the "Estimated Benefits" tab, you will see the amount of your monthly Social Security income if you take it at FRA, age 70, and anywhere in between. Please note that the annual statement and the Retirement Estimator do not factor COLAs into your age-70 benefit. This means your actual benefit will likely be higher than they indicate. Your retirement planner will have a calculator that will adjust for COLAs. If you know your PIA, a professional retirement planner can project your future benefits. You might also find one of the three calculators at the Social Security website useful. Go to www.ssa.gov/planners/benefitcalculators.htm and follow the cookie crumb trail.

What about Spousal Benefits?

Social Security was instituted in an earlier era, when most married women did not work, so to describe them requires me to break with 21st century protocol and step over the boundaries of political correctness a bit. Using the traditional frame of reference, spousal benefits were instituted to give women a measure of financial security in their old age. The spousal benefit is 50% of the worker's PIA if she applies for it at her full retirement age. If she applies at 62, it will be 35% of the worker's PIA. So let's say we have a couple here by the name of John, who is the primary worker, and Jane, who is his spouse. If John's PIA is $2,000 and Jane's PIA is $800, and if Jane applies for Social Security at her full retirement age, her benefit will equal 50% of John's PIA, or $1,000. This is $200 more than her benefit based on her own work record. Regardless of why these spousal benefits were put in place, there exist some innovative ways baby boomers may take advantage of them to make their retirement more secure.

Here are the basic rules for spousal benefits: (1) The primary worker must have filed for benefits. If he wants to delay his benefit until age 70 in order to receive a higher amount, he can file for benefits at his full retirement age and ask that they be suspended. (2) The low-earning spouse must be at least 62 for a reduced benefit or 66 for the full spousal benefit. (3) Spousal benefits do not earn delayed credits after age 66. Other questions about spousal benefits will be address in subsequent chapters of this book.

Divorced Spouse Benefits

One spouse can receive Social Security based on the work record of his or her former marriage partner, providing the marriage lasted 10 years or more and the spouse in question is currently unmarried. Yes, both husbands and wives can receive spousal benefits. Here are the basic rules for divorced-spouse benefits:

More than one ex-spouse can receive benefits on the same worker's record. So if your ex-husband has remarried a couple of times, all three ex-wives can claim divorced-spouse benefits, as long as the marriages lasted at least 10 years.

The benefits paid to one ex-spouse do not affect those paid to the worker, the current spouse, or the other ex-spouses.

The worker will not be notified that the ex-spouse has applied for benefits. So you need not worry that your long-lost ex-husband will find out that you applied for benefits based on his work record. You do not need to know the ex-spouse's whereabouts. You just have to have enough identifying information to enable the Social Security people to look up his records. You'll also need to provide documentation showing the dates of the marriage and divorce. Divorce benefits stop upon remarriage, but you may then be eligible for spousal benefits based on your new mate's work record. Or you may want to switch to your own benefit if you qualify for Social Security.

Survivor Benefits

The important thing to know about survivor benefits is that when one spouse dies, the surviving spouse receives the higher of the two benefits. Let's say Joe and Julie are married. Both currently receive Social Security benefits. Joe's benefit is $2,000 and Julie's benefit is $1,200. If Joe dies, Julie's $1,200 benefit will stop and she will start receiving $2,000. If Julie dies first, her $1,200 benefit will stop, and Joe will keep receiving his $2,000 benefit.

One important planning note: most widows and widowers need at least **two-thirds** of the amount of income they were receiving as a couple, so it is important to plan for the loss of one spouse's Social Security benefit. Even though it is the higher benefit that will be retained, the death of a spouse means the loss of one Social Security check.

Basic rules for survivor benefits are as follows: In order for the surviving spouse to receive survivor benefits, the marriage must have lasted at least nine months, except in the case of an accidental death. To start benefits, the survivor must be at least 60, or 50 if disabled. However, if the widow or widower applies before full retirement age, the benefit will be reduced, as it is for regular retirement benefits.

Some of the same principles that go into deciding when to apply for regular retirement benefits also apply to survivor benefits.

An Income You Can't Outlive

Most people tend to minimize the value of Social Security. Don't get me wrong. I realize that it is not the most significant piece of your retirement puzzle. If you think it is, then you may be in for a rude financial awakening once you retire. But it is a significant piece. Social Security is one of the few sources of income you can't outlive. If you are worried about running out of personal assets in your old age, you need not have that fear with Social Security because it continues until you die. And, of course, the longer you live, the more you will extract from the system. More education is needed, however, about the moving parts of Social Security, and how to ensure that we make the most of them for our retirement. (*Source for Social Security data: Savvy Social Security Seminar)*

Chapter Four

When Should I Take My Social Security?

Determining when to apply for Social Security is a big decision. As the overview in the previous chapter made clear, how much you receive in the way of Social Security benefits will depend on how and when you claim them. You can take your Social Security at age 62; you can wait until full retirement age, which is age 66 for most of you; or you can wait until you reach age 70. According to the findings of the National Bureau of Economic Research, most people take Social Security before age 65, well before they reach full retirement age. But is that the smart thing to do?

Here's another question. If you have money in qualified retirement accounts, such as traditional IRAs, 401(k) plans, 457 plans or 403 (b) plans, when should you begin withdrawing money from these accounts to support you in retirement? Most people, research shows, don't take money out of qualified plans until age 70½ when RMDs kick in. When choosing between taking early Social Security benefits or withdrawing money from qualified accounts, they will opt for early Social Security, when it is wiser to do just the opposite. You should actually take money out of your qualified plans before taking your Social Security. In fact, in most cases, it is wise to delay taking your Social Security until age 70.

One of the most fascinating research papers I have come across lately is a study produced in February 2012 by the National Bureau of

Economic Research entitled, "Were They Prepared for Retirement?" Written by James Poterba, Steven Venti and David A. Wise, it deals with the financial preparedness of older Americans. To the best of my knowledge, the NBER is an unbiased organization. The studies are conducted by professors with nothing to be gained by slanting the statistics one way or the other to prove a point or make a case. It is eye-opening. Here is an excerpt:

"We find that a substantial fraction of persons die with virtually no financial assets - 46.1% with less than $10,000 - and many of these households also have no housing wealth and rely almost entirely on Social Security benefits for support."

Did that statistic jump out at you like it jumped out at me? Almost 50% of Americans die virtually penniless and end up 100% dependent on Social Security? If that's the case, wouldn't it make more sense, if you have money in qualified accounts, to use that money first so it would enable you to postpone taking Social Security benefits until you are 70 years of age? That way your income would be nearly double, counting the delayed credits and the Cost of Living Adjustments. If you're going to spend your IRA money anyway, why delay?

The second part of the story is this: Taxes. Unless it's a Roth, the money that comes out of your qualified account is going to be taxable. There's no way around that. As this book is being written, taxes are low. The government can, and probably will, raise taxes in the future. If you are taking money from your qualified accounts and paying taxes on it now, you are probably receiving more favorable tax treatment than you will in the future.

At the time of this writing, the United States government is over $17.3 trillion dollars in debt and the clock is rolling. If you want to get an uneasy feeling about the future, just go to the website www.usdebtclock.org and watch the numbers roll up like a car odometer on amphetamines. If by chance the politicians regain a grip on reality and reverse the runaway debt, then there will be nothing to see, and that would mean the country is on the road to financial health. But don't hold your breath. As of this writing, there is over $16.8 trillion in Social Security unfunded liability, over $22.2 trillion in Part D Medicare Prescription Drug unfunded liability, and $88.4 trillion in

Medicare unfunded liability. Those three unfunded liabilities total over $127.4 trillion. Ouch! Bringing it closer to home, that's $1,107,086 per taxpayer, according to the website.

The word "trillion" rolls off the tongue so easily. It rhymes with "million" and "billion." But the leap from million to billion is nowhere near the jump to light speed that characterizes going from billion to trillion. It staggers the imagination to such a degree that we scramble for ways to express it. The following may help you wrap your mind around it:

What year was it a trillion seconds ago?

31,710 B.C.

If you spent $1 million per day, how long would it take to spend $1 trillion?

2,739 years.

To illustrate what a trillion dollars looks like, let's start with something we can understand.

This is a stack of $100 bills ½" thick, which adds up to $10,000.

This is what $1 million dollars (100 packets of $10,000) looks like. You could stuff that into a briefcase or large handbag and walk around with it.

Shown here is $1 trillion. It's a million million.
It's a thousand billion. It's a one followed by 12 zeros.
The man is that little speck over in the left side
of the illustration. The pallets have been double stacked
with 100 dollar bills and would fill a large warehouse.
Forget trying to haul this mass of cash anywhere.

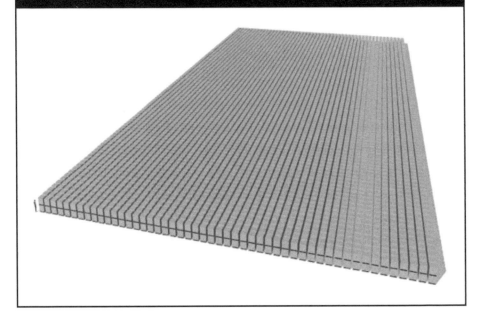

With all that debt and unfunded liability, what does the future hold? Perhaps a look into the past may give us a clue. The highest tax bracket ever recorded in American history between 1913 until now was 94%. In 1941, the highest tax bracket was 81% for anyone making over $5 million. The very next year it went up to 88%. But what did the IRS do? They lowered the threshold to $200,000. So not only did they increase taxes by 7%, they included way more people by reducing the threshold from $5 million to $200,000. There is more than one way to increase taxes. One is to raise the tax rates, which gets a lot of attention and is unpopular, and thus something politicians are loathe to do. The other way is to lower the threshold. That is what I call a "stealth tax increase." You don't see it coming.

Chapter Five

The Social Security
Break-Even Analysis

Sometimes during the retirement workshops I conduct, when I begin working through why I think it is wise to wait as long as possible before taking Social Security, I will try to elicit responses from the audience along the way with questions like: "What do you think?" and "Does this make sense?" and "Does everyone agree?" I am looking for someone who is of the opinion that it is wiser to take Social Security early. I know he or she is out there, and it's just a matter of time before, with sufficient encouragement, he/she will take exception to my remarks.

"No, Mark," says the dissenter. "You're wrong on this one. You see, I have done my own research and based on my findings, it makes more sense to take your Social Security at age 62. You end up with more money that way in the long run."

I know what they're thinking. They are looking at a simple break-even analysis. They are looking at the amount they would receive if they began taking Social Security at age 62, and extrapolating that out for, say 20 years, until age 82. Then, they are doing the same math, only this time starting their Social Security payments later at, say, age 70, and extrapolating that number out to the same age. Their calculations, if done that way, lead them to the inevitable conclusion that the extra money on the front end makes taking Social Security income at 62 the most appealing choice available to them. Generally, when people do that, the breakeven point is between 77 and 78 years of age.

I understand where they are coming from. But it's not that simple, especially if you have IRAs, 401(k)s or other qualified savings plans. There are other considerations that need to be included in the calculations. What type of investments do you have? What are the tax implications?

Let's do a typical break-even analysis. You are age 62. If you begin taking your Social Security payments now, your monthly payments would be $1,653. If you wait until age 70, your monthly check, allowing for a 2.8% COLA (cost of living adjustment), would be $3,628. If I add those numbers up until they "break even," or match each other the point is somewhere between age 77 and 78. Let's call taking your Social Security at age 62 "scenario one," and taking it at age 70 "scenario two." Under scenario one, if you live to age 85, you would have collected $666,027. Under scenario two, if you live to age 85, you would have collected $863,834. That's almost $197,807 more. If you have a spouse, just double that number. Over time, that's almost $400,000 more for a couple by choosing to take Social Security later rather than earlier. We didn't even figure in the spousal benefit that is available at age 66. That's when the lower income earning spouse will collect a spousal benefit on the higher income earning spouse. That would add another $50,000 to the equation, making for a total of almost a half-million dollars extra, just by postponing taking Social Security until age 70.

"Knowing that, why would anyone take Social Security early?" asks someone in the audience. Good question. Why would they?

The answer is because, whether on purpose or inadvertently, when Social Security benefits are explained to us there is often a certain "slant" put to it. The National Bureau of Economic Research (NBER) of Cambridge, Massachusetts, calls it "framing." In May 2011, the NBER produced a report that said "framing," or the way in which benefits are characterized and described, has a direct effect on "claim behavior," that is, how and when eligible individuals claim their benefits. The report, which was prepared by Jeffrey R. Brown, Arie

Kapteyn, and Olivia S. Mitchell, was entitled "Framing Effects and Expected Social Security Claiming Behavior." Here is an excerpt:

"Eligible participants in the U.S. Social Security system may claim benefits anytime from age 62-70, with benefit levels actuarially adjusted based on the claiming age. This paper shows that individual intentions with regard to Social Security claiming ages are sensitive to how the early versus late claiming decision is framed. Using an experimental design, we find that the use of a "break-even analysis" has the very strong effect of encouraging individuals to claim early. We also show that individuals are more likely to report they will delay claiming when later claiming is framed as a gain, and when the information provides an anchoring point at older, rather than younger, ages."

Did you catch that? Many people are influenced to claim their benefits because of the way the decision is "framed," or explained to them. If they are led to believe that it is in their best interest to claim it early, that is what they will decide to do. But when given an analysis and shown the facts, they may opt to claim them later.

What did the earlier NBER report reveal? That 46.1% of Americans will likely die while being 100% dependent upon Social Security? That statistic adds even more weight to the argument for waiting until age 70, or at least as long as possible, to take one's Social Security. If you have an IRA, taking proceeds from that account may enable you to do so.

The decision of when to apply for benefits is one of the most crucial decisions you will make as you approach retirement. It can literally make the difference of thousands of dollars over your lifetime. But there is no one-size-fits-all answer. Your decision will be uniquely yours, based on a number of factors. These include your health status, your life expectancy, your need for income, whether or not you plan to work and, if you are a surviving spouse, whether you have other personal resources.

The obvious advantage to delaying benefits is that your monthly benefit will be higher. Using the example of a baby boomer born in 1950 who had maximum earnings, he or she would receive $1,850 per month at age 62, but $3,255 if he/she waited until age 70. The difference becomes even more dramatic if we multiply these amounts by 2.8% annual COLAs. If cost-of-living adjustments average 2.8% over the next eight years, age-70 benefit jumps to $4,060. The chart below assumes a PIA at 62 of $2,466. Notice how much more income can be received by delaying Social Security as long as possible.

Age at which benefits are claimed	% of PIA	Benefit without COLAs	Benefit with COLAs
62	75	$1,850	$1,850
63	80	$1,973	$2,028
64	87	$2,137	$2,259
65	93	$2,302	$2,500
66	100	$2,466	$2,754
67	108	$2,663	$3,058
68	116	$2,861	$3,376
69	124	$3,058	$3,710
70	132	$3,255	$4,060

Let's not forget the cumulative effect of delaying Social Security. As the illustration below shows, the longer you live, the more income you will have.

Benefit at age	If claim at 62	If claim at 70
70	$2,307	$4,060
75	$2,649	$4,661
80	$3,041	$5,351
85	$3,492	$6,144
90	$4,008	$7,053
95	$4,602	$8,098
100	$5,283	$9,296

The "when to apply" question is very complex and really requires a customized analysis. But here are a few points to remember. If you apply early, your benefit starts out at some fraction of your PIA – 75% or 80% or whatever – and remains at that percentage for the rest of your life. It does not go up to 100% when you reach full retirement age.

COLAs magnify the impact of early or delayed retirement because the annual cost-of-living adjustment is applied to either the lower or higher amount. This causes the disparity to increase with each passing year. Finally, the "when to apply" question impacts survivor benefits as well. High-earning husbands, for instance, would be wise to delay benefits to age 70 if they can because that will give their wives the highest benefit after they die.

Chapter Six

When Working and
Social Security Don't Mix

You've been paying tax into the Social Security system for many years now. Every time you receive your paycheck, you look at the stub and your eyes scan to the place where the deductions are spelled out. You grimace. It pains you to think of all of the money you have earned that never reached your bank account or your pockets.

Rest assured you are not alone. American workers across the country go through the same emotions every payday.

On January 1, 2013, a lame duck Congress at the last minute voted to approve legislation that would avoid what the media dubbed the "fiscal cliff," a catchy term for the conundrum that the U.S. government would face at the end of 2012, when the terms of the Budget Control Act of 2011 were scheduled to go into effect.

With the precipice avoided, the maximum that employees and employers will now each pay in 2013 is $7,049.40, an increase of $2,425.20 for employees over the previous year and an increase of $223.20 for employers.

Other important measures approved include:

Social Security: The new Wage Base was increased to $113,700, an increase of $3,600 from the previous wage base of $110,100. As before, there is no limit to the wages subject to the Medicare tax; therefore all covered wages are still subject to the 1.45% tax.

Medicare: Taxable Medicare wages paid in excess of $200,000 are subject to an extra 0.9% Medicare tax that will only be withheld from employees' wages. Employers will not pay the extra tax.

The Bush (President George W.) era payroll tax cut expired, resulting in 2% more in employee Social Security tax withholding. For the time being, the employer rate remains 6.2 percent. The Medicare rate, also matched by the employer, is unchanged at 1.45 percent and applies to all wages.

But since there is nothing we can do about any of it, except write our congressional representative, most Americans just wonder, "When do we stop giving and start taking?" This may be why many make the mistake of taking their Social Security checks as soon as possible. We have already made the case that starting Social Security at 62, while it may be emotionally satisfying, is not usually prudent. If you know how Social Security works, you'll realize that there are two reasons why starting at the opening bell is, more often than not, a bad idea:

* **Before your "full retirement age," working and Social Security benefits don't mix well.** If you have even moderate amounts of earned income, your Social Security checks will be reduced or eliminated altogether.

* **Even if you're not working, starting at 62 or soon afterwards cuts the amount you'll receive for the rest of your life.** Uncle Sam provides generous incentives to wait as long as possible – until age 70 – to start collecting your benefits.

Labor Pains

Social Security has had an earnings penalty (now called by the more acceptable term "earnings test") since the 1930s. The rules were changed in 2000. Today's rules are more favorable to seniors who wish to keep working, but they're a little complicated.

For the earnings test, seniors fall into one of three categories:

1. **Those who have not yet reached the year of their full retirement age (FRA).** At this writing, the FRA is 66. That applies to people born from 1943 through 1954. If you were born after 1954, FRA increases

gradually to 66 and two months, 66 and four months, etc. If you were born in 1960 or later, your FRA is 67.

2. Those who are in the calendar year of reaching their FRA, but not there yet. Suppose Art Young was born in June 1949. His FRA is 66, an age he'll reach in June 2015. Thus, Art is in the first category in 2011, 2012, 2013 and 2014. From January through May of 2015, Art is in the second category.

3. Those who have reached their FRA. In June 2015, Art will reach his FRA and move into the third category, where he'll stay for the rest of his life.

While you are in category one, you face a severe loss of Social Security benefits if you're still earning income. If you are younger than full retirement age during all of 2013, the government will deduct $1 from your benefits for each $2 you earned above $15,120. That ceiling was $14,640 the year before. Once you reach your FRA, however, you can earn any amount and still receive your full benefit.

Note that these limits apply only to income from working. You can have any amount of income from interest, dividends or capital gains and still collect the Social Security benefit to which you're entitled, as long as you don't go over the earnings limits.

Now, it's true that this reduction in earnings is not permanent. If some of your Social Security retirement benefits are withheld because of your earnings, your benefits will be increased starting at your full retirement age to take into account those months in which benefits were withheld. Nevertheless, these earnings tests make it less appealing to start benefits before your FRA, if you have earnings.

What if you put your earnings toward a 401(k)? Doesn't matter. The Social Security checks will still be smaller. Yes, your contributions to the 401(k) will lower your taxable income, but it's still your gross wages from a job or self-employment – before any deductions for taxes or 401(k) contributions – that determine whether your Social Security benefits will be reduced under the earnings cap.

The 8% Solution

From age 62 until your FRA, another set of rules will reduce your Social Security benefits, and this reduction will be permanent. In essence, the earlier you start, the smaller the benefit you'll receive. At the time of this writing, if you start at 62, your monthly check will be only 75% of the benefit you would have received at age 66.

Suppose Beth Williams was born in 1951 so she'll be 62 in 2013. If she starts Social Security benefits this year, the Social Security Administration will determine what her FRA would be if Beth decided to wait until her FRA. Beth will get 75% of that amount.

Say that Beth's FRA benefit is calculated at $2,000 a month. By starting at age 62, she would get $1,500 a month – a 25% reduction in monthly income. That's the amount Beth will receive for the rest of her life, plus any cost-of-living adjustments (COLAs).

The longer Beth waits to start benefits, the larger each check will be. She will get 80% of her FRA benefit if she starts at age 63, for example, and 86.7% if she starts at age 64.

The bottom line is that Beth (and everyone else born from 1943 through 1954) will increase her benefits by 33.3% by waiting from age 62 to age 66 to start. Instead of $1,500 a month (plus COLAs), Beth will receive $2,000 a month for the rest of her life, plus any COLAs. Thus, Beth gets a 33.3% boost in lifetime income by waiting four years to start. **That's a return of around 8% a year**, on the money not requested.

I just saw a light bulb go off over many heads out there. When you think of it as a passive return on investment, it puts delaying Social Security benefits in an entirely new light. Once Beth reaches age 66, her FRA, she can earn any amount, without any reduction in benefits. There's no reduction for starting early, either. Therefore, Beth faces no obstacles to starting her retirement benefits then.

That doesn't mean Beth should start her benefits at her FRA. After your FRA, Social Security offers a "delayed retirement credit" of 8% a year. (Actually, the credit is 2/3% per month, after your FRA). This goes on until you reach age 70, after which there is no point in waiting any longer. Thus, anyone who reaches his or her FRA at age 66 will get a monthly check that's 8% larger by starting at age 67, 16% larger at 68, 24% larger at 69, and 32% larger at 70.

Beth Williams, in this example, could increase her monthly check from $1,500 a month to $2,640 a month, by waiting from age 62 to age 70. She'll collect that larger benefit, plus COLAs, until she dies. What's more, waiting is an especially attractive strategy for a married couple. After one spouse dies, the surviving spouse will receive the higher of two benefits: the survivor's monthly benefit or the deceased spouse's benefit.

Suppose, for example, that Charlie Thomas waits until age 70 to start his benefits. He collects those benefits for nearly 20 years, until he is receiving more than $4,000 a month at the time of his death. Charlie's wife Diane, who had not earned substantial amounts in her career, receives about $2,000 a month then, in this example.

After Charlie dies, Diane will collect the higher benefit – Charlie's $4,000-plus per month – for the rest of her life. Thus, for couples where the higher-earning spouse has a shorter life expectancy, a delay in starting benefits by the higher-earner acts as a form of life insurance, payable to the surviving spouse.

Waiting until you are 70 years of age may not be possible for everyone. What if you **absolutely** need the money for living expenses? Then go ahead. Start your Social Security retirement benefits as soon as you can. If you have a serious health condition, you might as well start receiving benefits early, to collect while you can. Otherwise, if you are in reasonably good health – or married to a spouse with a longer life expectancy – and you have other assets you can use for spending money, it pays to wait. Uncle Sam is promising you an 8% return, with no investment risk, government-guaranteed. If you have to cash in low-yielding assets to live on, consider doing so in order to earn that 8% a year, in addition to COLAs, until you reach age 70.

Chapter Seven

A Dollar Saved for
Retirement Is Really Five

John Doe is 53 years old. He works at a warehouse and earns $40,000 per year before taxes. He has a 401(k) program at work, but he hasn't contributed to it like he should and the program has no matching funds. The last time John checked his statement there was less than $4,000 in the plan. He knows he should save more, but he finds it difficult to do on his salary. John is divorced and pays child support for his son from the failed marriage. Between his apartment rent, car payment and the $12,000 he owes in credit card debt, he can hardly afford to set aside money for retirement.

John is, of course, fictional. But his situation reflects that of many Americans who feel as if their retirement future is uncertain. Unless John lands a job with a higher paying salary, or comes up with some cash from an inheritance or wins the power ball lottery, he will likely limp along until retirement and then collect his Social Security. Like millions of other Americans, John's main source of income will be his Social Security check when he retires.

Of course, it all depends on your highest 35 earnings years as to how much your personal Social Security check will be, but according to the U.S. Social Security Administration, the average monthly Social Security benefit for a retired worker was about $1,230 at the beginning of 2012. So, if John is going to get by in retirement, he has to do a couple of things that may be distasteful to him. One is to continue working as long as possible – perhaps years after the normal retirement age. Another is to establish and abide by a tight budget. John could also consider working a second part-time job to boost his income. That would enable him to actively save money for retirement and passively save money by increasing the amount he pays into the system. Improving your earnings record can increase the amount of your monthly Social Security check.

This nail is already in the plank, but I will hammer it once more just for emphasis – John will find it to his advantage to wait until he is age 70 to begin taking his Social Security so he can get the maximum obtainable from the system.

Mr. Doe should also go to the website discussed in Chapter One, secure.ssa.gov/RIL/SiView.do, and create an account so he can get an estimate of how much his Social Security payments will be when he retires. First, check your annual statement to make sure your earnings record is accurate. Mistakes are rare because the earnings kept on file at Social Security were reported by employers when they submitted your Social Security taxes. But mistakes can happen, especially for self-employed individuals, whose earnings records are taken from tax returns.

Even if you start receiving Social Security and continue to work, your earnings record will be updated. He should also realize that, because of the double-edged sword of compound interest, every dollar he puts on a credit card (unless he pays his balance in full each month) is five dollars he will not have in retirement. Let's say that he wants to buy a new car. He must realize that he can either have a new car, the payments for which will last six years and require him to pay at least one-third of the purchase price in interest, or he can save the value of that new car for his future. But he certainly cannot do both.

Budget for Retirement

One way to enhance your retirement is by starting as soon as possible to live within your means. Scratch that. Live a notch or two **below** your means. Take the money you save by doing so and apply it to your future. Learning to separate needs from wants may be a factor here. Living below your means but within your needs is simple. It may not always be easy, but it is simple. If your car is a 6-year-old Ford and it gets you where you want to go, then keep it. Put another 100,000 miles on it. Don't buy a new BMW just because your credit score will allow you to do it, or just because the loan officer at the dealership says he can get you a seven-year loan. If you can afford to buy a 3,000-square-foot home, buy a 2,000-square-foot home. Sure, you would like to blow $5,000 on that resort vacation you've been dreaming of. You don't have to chuck it...just postpone it until you are paying for it with extra money, not money you should be saving for retirement.

I know some people who have started what they call "retirement gardens" to reduce food costs. You would be amazed at how much money you can save with tomatoes at a dollar each. With the new digital age, many are looking into ways to cut out duplicative phone and television services. Do you really need all the entertainment you treat yourself to? When there are free concerts in the park and movies at the one-dollar box at the grocery store?

Can you see yourself saving $10 a day? Let me put it another way. Do you waste $10 a day on things you don't really need? I thought so. Did you know that if you took that $10 and saved it in a piggy bank, at the end of 20 years you would have $73,000? However, what if you could get a measly 6% interest? Your monthly deposit of $300 for 20 years with an interest rate of 6.00% compounded annually would, after 20 years, yield $136,993.73. There are all manner of strategies to which you could put that money to work during retirement to make it last the rest of your life.

Controlling the cost of housing may be a challenge, but many Americans are paying far too much of their monthly income for rent or mortgage payments. You might have also heard that you should spend no more than 30% of your annual income on rent or mortgage payments. It may buy you a few extra square feet of living space, and perhaps a bit more prestige, but it leaves your flank unprotected if you are unable to save for retirement. Spending 30% of your yearly income on rent is widely believed to be an affordable amount, leaving enough money for all your other expenses. Some pay much more than that and, hence, are unable to save for retirement.

When the housing bubble burst in 2007 and property values plummeted, many homeowners learned a bitter lesson. Spending a greater portion of one's income than is traditionally prudent with the idea that home values will always go up can backfire. Rent and mortgage debt is one of your largest expenses. When you're working on a manageable budget to accommodate a more comfortable retirement, it is definitely a major category to consider possible adjustments. There are some unexpected advantages to downsizing. In addition to the obvious – lower rent – property taxes and maintenance expenses will also be lowered.

Americans who are homeowners have an ace in the hole when it comes to retirement – maybe. If you own a home and you have equity in that home, then it is an asset you can fall back on if necessary. Is it a liquid asset? Hardly. But it can be turned into cash in a variety of ways.

In some cases where the homeowner is retired and at least age 62, with no mortgage, or only a small amount left on a mortgage balance, he or she may be eligible for a reverse mortgage. In general, I am not a proponent of reverse mortgages unless all other options have been pursued. Because reverse mortgages are equity loans, they typically come with higher fees than traditional mortgages. But this type of loan generally does not require repayment as long as you continue to live in that home for the rest of your life, keep up the house, and pay the property taxes. However, if you later wish to move, you must repay the lender the principal value of the loan, plus interest and fees. And only the equity remaining in the home after the loan is completely repaid will be passed on to your heirs.

If your *future* self could hang out with your *now* self for a while, what do you think they would talk about? If you planned well, you might get thanked for all the work you did back then that made your future so worry-free. But if you are one of those people who either procrastinates for one of 50 reasons (and you know what they are) or one who just likes to let "life happen," then your future self may have some criticism for the way you handled things. A little planning now can make a world of difference in the years to come, as subsequent chapters will show.

Chapter Eight

Strategies for Maximizing
Your Social Security Benefits

When I was in junior high school, I decided I would learn to play chess. It was sort of a fad sweeping the eighth grade. I thought the best way to learn the game was to play with another classmate who already knew the game. I figured chess couldn't be much more complicated than checkers. After all, they were played on the same board. I knew the basic pieces and how they moved. It looked like fun. The other kid slaughtered me. It was checkmate in fewer than 10 moves every time we played – that is, until I bought a little 50-cent book entitled *Chess for Beginners* at the local news stand and learned that there was something called "strategy" that was involved in this game. Once I understood the rules and strategy, I rocked! Well, that may be overstating it a bit. At least I didn't get killed so much.

When it comes to collecting Social Security, there are certain strategies, all perfectly legal and ethical, and even approved by the Social Security Administration, that, when employed, can result in a maximization of benefits to the tune of thousands. Making the proper "moves" at the proper time can help Social Security recipients, couples especially, get the most out of the system while they are still alive and maximize income for survivors after death. Some of these strategies can be a little complicated. What follows are a few examples along with illustrations as to how they work.

"File and Suspend"

One strategy, perfectly legal and acceptable to the government but one not known commonly, is called "file and suspend" or "claim and suspend," depending on which financial advisor language you speak. The concept comes out of the Center for Retirement Research at Boston College. Here's the way it works:

At FRA (full retirement age), a higher-earning spouse applies for his Social Security benefit and asks that it be suspended.

- The lower-earning spouse files for spousal benefit.
- The higher-earning spouse claims benefits at age 70.

Consider the case of Bob and Barbara:

- Bob and Barbara are both age 66
- Bob's Primary Insurance Amount (PIA) is $2,000; Barbara's PIA is $800 (less than her spousal benefit of $1,000)
- If Bob waits until age 70 to apply, his benefit will increase to $2,640. However, Barbara may not claim her spousal benefit until Bob files for benefits
- Bob "files and suspends" at 66. This entitles Barbara to her spousal benefit, while Bob's benefit continues to earn delayed credits.
- A word of caution: "File and suspend" may not be done before full retirement age.

Something to remember: In order for a low-earning spouse to receive a spousal benefit, the high-earning spouse **must** have filed for benefits. But often the high-earning spouse wants to delay his benefit to age 70 in order to maximize income to the couple while both are alive, and income to the surviving spouse after one spouse dies. So as soon as the high-earning spouse turns full retirement age, he files for his benefit and then immediately suspends it. This allows his wife to start her spousal benefit while his benefit earns 8% annual delayed credits, plus COLAs.

Please note that this does not work if Bob is under full retirement age. It is only after full retirement age that a person may voluntarily suspend their benefit in order to earn delayed credits. The lower-earning spouse may, of course, apply for her spousal benefit at any time after the age of 62. If she applies before full retirement age, she will receive a lower amount. In order to receive the full 50% of her husband's PIA, she must apply at full retirement age.

Claim Now, Claim More Later

Here's another strategy that has come out of the Center for Retirement Research at Boston College. It's called "claim now, claim more later," and it has been blessed by the Social Security Administration, even if all the local Social Security personnel are not quite up to speed on it. At full retirement age, the higher earning spouse may apply for his or her spousal benefit only. The other spouse must be receiving benefits on her record. Then, at age 70, the higher earning spouse switches to his or her own higher benefit.

Here's an example:
- Mike and Mary are both age 66
- Mike's Primary Insurance Amount (PIA) is $2,000
- Mary's PIA is $800
- Mary files for her benefit at age 66
- Mike files for his spousal benefit at the same time and begins collecting $400 (half of Mary's PIA)
- When Mike turns 70, he switches to his own higher benefit.
- Result: Mike receives an additional $400 per month from age 66-70

Here are a few cautions you will want to take note of regarding the "claim now, claim more later" strategy.
- Higher-earning spouses may not do this before FRA
- Only one spouse may do this (both spouses can't be receiving spousal benefits at the same time)

- Spousal planning analysis can determine which of the various spousal strategies will work best for your unique situation

It is important to follow the rules carefully, or this strategy could backfire. First, you cannot do it before full retirement age. If Mike walks into his Social Security office before he turns 66, they will compare his own benefit to his spousal benefit and give him the higher of the two. He will be given his own benefit, and it will be reduced for early claiming. It is only after full retirement age that he can "restrict" his application to his spousal benefit. And that's the language he should use. Social Security personnel are accustomed to giving people the highest benefit they are entitled to, but if he restricts his application to his spousal benefit, his own higher benefit will not be part of the application. That way, it can continue to earn delayed credits until he turns 70.

Another important note is that both spouses cannot do this. The explanation is complicated, but suffice it to say that if one spouse is claiming spousal benefits, the other spouse must be receiving benefits on his or her own record. And finally, spousal strategies may vary depending on the ages and PIAs of the respective spouses. At our office, we use a special Spousal Planning Calculator that will help us analyze the possible strategies for each individual situation so we can devise a plan that will be custom fitted to each individual's circumstances.

Chapter Nine

Minimizing Taxes on Social Security

In 1935, when President Franklin D. Roosevelt signed the Social Security Act into law, it is claimed that he vowed never to tax Social Security Benefits. FDR kept his promise, too, because as long as he was alive, there was no tax imposed on Social Security benefits. But during Ronald Reagan's presidency, the Social Security Amendments of 1983 changed all of that. Beginning in 1984, if your base income as a single taxpayer was $25,000, or, if you earned more than $32,000 per year as a married couple filing jointly, then up to 50% of your Social Security could be taxed by the Internal Revenue System.

The next tax increase would come with the 1993 budget deal under President Bill Clinton, which raised taxation to up to 85% of benefits for single filers with incomes of more than $34,000, and for couples with annual incomes of $44,000 or more.

It still comes as a surprise to some that if they exceed the earnings ceiling, they will have to pay income taxes on Social Security benefits. Keep in mind, however, that there are strategies that can be used to limit, or perhaps even eliminate, Social Security taxes. It all depends on how much other income you have as to how much of your Social Security Benefits will be taxed and at what rate.

"Income" in this case means provisional income, which includes adjusted gross income, plus one-half of the Social Security benefit, plus any tax-exempt interest. If provisional income is under $32,000 for a married couple, no benefits are subject to tax. If provisional income is between $32,000 and $44,000, up to 50% of a married couple's benefits are subject to tax. If provisional income is over $44,000, up to 85% of benefits are subject to tax. The thresholds for a single individual are $25,000 and $34,000. In the case of married filing separately and living with spouse, 85% of Social Security is taxable regardless of income level.

Filing Status	Provisional Income	Amount of SS subject to tax
Married filing jointly	Under $32,000 $32,000 - $44,000 Over $44,000	0 50% 85%
Single, head of household, qualifying widow(er), married filing separately & living apart from spouse	Under $25,000 $25,000 - $34,000 Over $34,000	0 50% 85%
Married filing separately and living with spouse	Over 0	85%

*Provisional income = AGI + one-half of SS benefit + tax-exempt interest

You can minimize taxes on Social Security by lowering your other income, *especially investment income*. But you should be aware that municipal bond interest, which is usually tax free, counts as income for the purpose of calculating the tax on Social Security benefits. Also, it's important to look ahead and plan for required minimum distributions from IRAs. Whether you like it or not, these can raise your taxable income and cause your Social Security benefits to be subject to tax. Please consult with your own tax advisor about your individual situation.

"Wait a minute, Mark...did you just say I should *lower* my investment income?" Allow me to explain. What we are doing here is *maximizing* income and *minimizing* taxes. So of course I don't mean to lower your income. But there's income that is reportable, or *considered* to be provisional income by the IRS, and there is income that is *not considered* reportable as provisional income by the IRS. We are talking about moving money from a non-tax-favored category to one that is favored. One way to accomplish this is to place assets in tax-deferred accounts, where the interest received is not considered to be income by the IRS, and is therefore not reportable. Gains paid on annuity balances, for example, are tax-deferred. So those gains are not reported as income on form 1040. This is not the case with interest earned by CDs and gains from mutual funds. They are fully reportable and taxable. Of course, any gains received within the annuity will eventually be taxed. This strategy is simply moving money from the *reportable* side of the ledger to the *non-reportable* side to keep down the exposure of Social Security payments to taxation. It is always wise to consult your own tax professional before making any significant changes.

Synchronize Your Retirement Income

Look at your retirement income picture as a machine with several moving parts that, in order to run smoothly, must all be synchronized. Social Security is one important cog in the machinery, but it must be considered in the context of all of your other retirement sources, including pensions, IRAs, 401(k)s, and RMDs (required minimum distributions) that will automatically join the income stream when you reach age 70 ½. Then there are your plans for working in retirement. Many Americans are choosing to continue working well past the age of 65, either because they love their jobs, own their own businesses, or need the income. Whatever the case, this needs to be a part of your retirement planning. The goal is to coordinate all of these resources so they will continue providing income for the rest of your life.

Planning is easy during your younger years. There are fewer dots to connect. Stash as much as possible from your paycheck into your 401(k). One of the biggest mistakes I see young people make is not taking full advantage of employer matching programs at their places of employment. If the boss is willing to match your contributions, even a little, that is free money. Take it.

When you near retirement and it is time to convert your nest egg into a life-long income stream, planning is essential. Ask for professional help at this stage of the game. A competent financial advisor who specializes in retirement income planning is like that capable machinist who knows how all the gears work, and he or she can set your retirement income picture to function like a well-oiled perpetual motion machine.

Chapter Ten

Social Security and Your Taxes

People love finding money. In fact, as a financial planner, nothing gives me more satisfaction than to find money for them – riches they didn't know they possessed.

When the conversation lags at a dinner party, one way to get it going again is by asking people to relate their personal answer to the question: "What was the largest amount of money you have ever found at one time?" The answers can be fascinating. Everyone, it seems, has a "found money" story. Some will tell about scrounging for coins in the family sofa, or the back seat of the family sedan. Others have found money in old wallets, or envelopes filled with cash while cleaning out a desk drawer, or $20 bills in wastebaskets. Personally, the most I have ever found was a $10 bill in an old jacket pocket. One friend, however, said he found two one-hundred dollar bills on the floor of a hotel restroom. He said his first inclination was to find the rightful owner. Then he said he realized how fruitless that search would likely be, so he decided he would pocket the money but use it for a worthy cause. I was eager to know what the worthy cause turned out to be, but someone else at the party interrupted him to tell their story and the conversation moved along.

Finding cash is exciting. Why? Because it is a surprise. Regardless of the amount, you just feel lucky the rest of the day.

As a financial planner, I often find money "hiding in plain sight" on forms and documents, disguised as either would-be tax obligations that disappear when certain strategies are employed, or better returns on money that is either unemployed or under employed. It is quite rewarding to see the smile of recognition form on clients' faces when they realize they are in possession of an asset they didn't know they had.

Saving money is the same as finding money. I love spotting a tax that would have been paid had we not found and pointed out an IRS provision that served to mitigate that perceived obligation. Bing! It's like spotting that $100 bill on the sidewalk.

Most clients with whom I work tell me they don't mind paying their fair share of taxes; they just don't want to pay *more* than their fair share. I am especially gratified when I am able to help retired clients find ways to legally and ethically avoid overpaying taxes because, more than any other segment of the population, seniors need their assets.

One of the first places I look when I'm searching for this found money in client's tax returns is a simple form that is published by the IRS, but is seldom seen. In fact, when I examine tax returns, I rarely see this form included in the packet. It is a worksheet, actually, that is not meant to be submitted with your tax returns, but should be kept with the file. It's called, appropriately enough, the "Figuring Your Taxable Benefits" worksheet. It has been my observation that people who do their own taxes often do not know this form exists, and many CPAs are not aware of it, either. Yet, it is this form that (a) helps you determine how much of your Social Security is taxable according to IRS regulations, and (b) helps you determine if there are ways to legally avoid paying that tax.

Before I go any further, let me pause here and explain something. Whenever I use the two words "avoid" and "tax" in the same sentence, I can see a few eyebrows arch upward. But there is a big difference between tax *avoidance* and tax *evasion.* What is the difference? Oh, about 10 to 20 years (bada bump...but seriously, folks...). Please rest assured, dear reader, that there is absolutely nothing improper, illegal, unethical or un-American about taking advantage of the provisions found in the IRS Code that enable us to position our assets in such a way as to eliminate unnecessary taxation. Keep in mind, there are 5.6 million words in the IRS code – about seven times as many as the Bible. If you are looking for chapter and verse on how to reduce your taxes, however, you won't find a large subheading in the IRS code entitled "How to Reduce Taxes." The language is buried among all the other words and phrases. You have to know what you're looking for to find it.

You can find this worksheet on the web. It is publication 915, entitled Social Security and Equivalent Railroad Retirement Benefits, and can be found at www.irs.gov/pub/irs-pdf/p915.pdf. Once you locate worksheet, go to line one. It will read: "Enter the total amount from box 5 of ALL your Forms SSA – 1099 & RRB 1099." That's essentially the 1099 you get from the government stating how much Social Security income you received that year. The letters RRB stand for Railroad Retirement Board. It's a long story as to why, but it means practically the same thing. What goes on that line is the total you received.

Line two tells you to divide that number in half and enter it in the blank provided. Then you are asked to add that figure (the one on line two) to all of your other income and move it over to the blank provided at the end of line three. That is going to be the amount you will pay taxes on. Notice that all other forms of income are listed dollar-for-dollar. But when it comes to your Social Security, the formula calls for only half of the total amount you received when figuring up your tax liability. In IRS speak, this is called the *combined income formula.*

Why are this form and this formula so important? Let me share with you the findings reported in *Recalibrating Retirement Spending and Saving* by John Ameriks and Olivia S. Mitchell. In chapter seven, there appears a very detailed discussion entitled "Rethinking Social Security Claiming in a 401(k) World." This piece of research was completed in August 2007 by James I. Mhaney and Peter C. Carlson for the Wharton School. Here's an excerpt:

> *"The Combined Income formula includes all of a retiree's income excluding Roth income together with 50 percent of their Social Security income. The amount of Social Security that is taxable is the minimum of three tests: 50 percent of the Combined Income amount*

over the first threshold plus 35 percent of Combined Income over the 2nd threshold, or 50 percent of benefits plus 85 percent of Combined Income over the 2nd threshold, or 85 percent of benefits. Combined Income counts all of the income that is normally taxable plus tax-free municipal bond income. Therefore a married couple which has saved diligently within a 401(k) can face a very high marginal tax rate on an additional dollar of IRA income. If the spouses are in a 25 percent tax bracket, they may pay 25 cents on the IRA dollar as ordinary income tax and another 21.25 cents on the Social Security dollar now subject to taxation at 85 percent ($1 x .85 x 25 percent). The effective marginal tax rate on that dollar is therefore 46.25 percent.

"State taxes can push the marginal tax rate even higher. Some financial journalists have dubbed this concept the "tax torpedo". But just as the tax torpedo can accelerate the taxes due on a retirement income strategy, trading IRA income for Social Security income can create a reverse tax torpedo and drastically reduce taxes."

Trading IRA income for Social Security income can create a **reverse tax torpedo**...that will **drastically** reduce your taxes in retirement. Don't forget that earlier statistic: 46.1% of all people die dependent solely on Social Security income. The report continues:

"Many of these retirees will find themselves hit by the tax torpedo. Contrast, however, an individual who delays taking Social Security and funds his needs out of his IRA or other qualified plan is, in essence, trading IRA income for higher Social Security income. This can provide distinct and measurable tax advantages. In lieu of just assuming that 85 percent of Social Security income will become taxable, it is important to recognize what type of income is being received. Since Social

Security income only counts at a 50 percent rate into the Combined Income formula, much larger amounts of Social Security can be received before the Combined Income thresholds are met. Therefore, when trading an IRA dollar of income for a Social Security dollar, not only is the IRA dollar no longer present (and thus no tax is due), but less Social Security income is also subject to taxation.

"A quick illustration is as follows: assume an IRA dollar is removed from the income pool and is added back in the form of Social Security. Removing the IRA dollar causes the Adjusted Gross Income to reduce by one dollar. Adjusted Gross Income (AGI) is income including wages, interest, capital gains, and income from retirement accounts adjusted downward by specific deductions (including contributions to deductible retirement accounts); but not including standard and itemized deductions. The IRA dollar being removed also causes Combined Income to drop by a dollar. The Social Security dollar that is added back counts only half to Combined Income, netting a 50 cent decrease in the Combined Income amount. If, for example, we assume that the Combined Income amount is already over the 2nd threshold, that 50 cent decrease results in an additional 42.5 cent reduction to Adjusted Gross Income (AGI). This results in a total AGI reduction of $1.425. The total gross income has not changed, but AGI is reduced by $1.425. In a 25 percent bracket, this saves $0.35625 in federal taxes on that dollar of income. If the beneficiary's state of residence also taxes Social Security, it functions the exact same way, albeit just with different tax rates. If the state does not tax Social Security, the lower IRA income still reduces state taxes. Of course, when enough dollars are shifted to Social Security (from an IRA), the retiree may slide into a marginal tax bracket *lower than 25 percent. Therefore, additional retirement income such as Required Minimum Distribution amounts may also benefit from lower tax rates. Of course, additional income could be subject to the "tax torpedo" as well.*

"Table 3 shows an example with $69,000 of pre-tax income. For a retired married couple both age 72, having Social Security income of $24,000 plus IRA income of $45,000 results in Adjusted Gross Income of $62,050. Conversely, the couple who delays Social Security and has Social Security income of $39,000 with a lower IRA income of $30,000 has the same pre-tax income of $69,000 but an adjusted gross income of only $40,675. The first couple has $21,375 more in Adjusted Gross Income – 52.5 percent higher and spends $3,206.25 more in federal income taxes."

Over a lifetime, folks, that can amount to hundreds of thousands of dollars. We actually had an accountant come in and crunch the numbers on sample tax returns just to check out these findings and see how they hold up in real-life situations. It all checks out. We even did some "what-if" returns. One couple had $97,000 in income and they took their Social Security early. By the time they were age 70, they were receiving $40,006 in total Social Security income between the two of them. They also had $56,994 they were taking out of their IRA and other investments. Based on the Combined Income Formula on the Social Security worksheet, $34,005 of their $40,000 in Social Security benefits would be taxable. Under that scenario, their Adjusted Gross Income (AGI) would be $90,999 and their tax liability would be $9,487.

But what would have happened if they had **delayed** taking their Social Security until age 70. They would have received $70,411 in Social Security benefits as a couple. They are taking $26,589 from their IRA investments. Under this scenario, of the $70,411, only $21,125 is taxable. They increased their Social Security by $30,405 and decreased the taxable portion of it by $12,880. Now, their AGI is $47,714 instead of $90,999. Their taxes owed amount to $2,995 instead of $9,487 – that's $6,492 lower taxes. The result of this "what-if" return was simply this: Same exact income = lower taxes.

Married Filing Jointly

Let's say we have a couple who is Married Filing Jointly using a standard 1040 Tax Return form. Together they earn an adjusted gross income of $70,000 per year. As MFJ filers, they are able to claim a combined $11,900 standard deduction and claim their two personal exemptions of $3,800 each that allows them to deduct $7,600 from their AGI. Their taxable income is now $50,500 and they will pay $6,683 in federal income taxes.

But what happens if one spouse dies? Because women tend to live longer than men by a couple of years, let's say it's the husband who passes away. Obviously the surviving spouse must now file as a single individual. Note on the whiteboard below under the column "SINGLE," we see that the adjusted gross income for the wife is still $70,000, but she may only claim half of the MFJ standard deduction ($5,950) and only one personal exemption ($3,800), which, when subtracted from the $70,000, results in an AGI of $60,250. Because the wife must now use the single tax rates, her taxes owed will be $10,991, even though her income remained the same after the husband died. That's an increase of $4,308, or a 64.46% tax increase following the death of a spouse.

Now on the last column over on our whiteboard, let's say the same situation exists – surviving spouse must file as single person with half the standard deduction and personal exemptions as before – but this time, let's say that for some reason, her income goes down to $60,000 AGI (14.29% less). Perhaps she lost a portion of his pension when he died. If the husband and wife are both on Social Security, and the husband dies, she will lose one of those incomes. She is able to retain the higher income, but the other income was a substantial part of her living. Subtracting the standard deduction and personal exemption, her AGI comes in at $50,250. Her taxes on that amount are $8,491. She had 14.29% less income but her taxes increased by $1,808, or 27.05%.

Family Taxes Before & After Death

Married Filing Jointly	2012 1040 Tax Return	Single	Single
$70,000	Adjusted Gross Income	$70,000	$60,000
− 11,900	Standard Deduction	−5,950	−5,950
− 7,600	Exemptions	−3,800	−3,800
$50,500	Taxable Income Line 43	$60,250	$50,250
$6,683	Tax	$10,991	$8,491
	Spouse Dies	Income Same	Income Decreased by $10,000
	% Change In Income	0%	↓ 14.29%
	Taxable Income	↑ $9,750	↓ $250
	Tax	↑ $4,308	↑ $1,808
	% Change In Tax	↑ 64.46%	↑ 27.05%

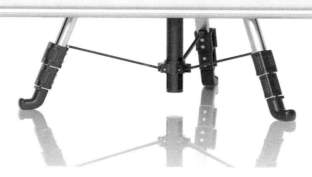

This is why couples need to plan for these contingencies while they are together. If you want to pull money out of a qualified plan, or if you have a decrease in income for any reason, the taxes are going to be lower if you are filing jointly than they will be if you are single. Keep in mind, that when your income increases, you can jump from one tax bracket to the next higher tax bracket. Proper planning would dictate that you keep your income below the threshold that would trigger that tax rate change if at all possible. A competent retirement income specialist can help you manage those thresholds and often enable you to avoid paying unnecessary taxes.

Chapter Eleven

Actual Versus Average Returns

S top me if you've heard this one: It's 1959. Three tired traveling salesmen stop at a hotel for the night. It's late and there is only one room left. They ask how much. The manager says $30 for the room. They agree to take it and split the cost. Each man puts a $10 dollar bill on the counter. They get the key and go to their room.

The manager notices that he made a mistake; the room is only $25 not $30. He gives five $1 dollar bills to a bellboy and instructs him to refund the men $5.00. As the bellboy rides the elevator up to the floor, he begins thinking. How can he give five dollars to three people? So he gets a bright idea. He gets to the room and gives each man one dollar back and keeps two for himself. So let's see, now...

> Each man (3) spent $9 = $27
> The assistant kept $2
> That's a total of $29!

What happened to the other dollar?

It's just a mathematical sleight-of-hand. It's like the guy who holds up his hands and says, "I have 11 fingers, see?" Then he begins to count them off, 10, nine, eight, seven, six and five makes 11!

These are harmless little math riddles, but when it comes to how some financial advisors like to point to **averages** instead of **actual** returns when predicting the behavior of your portfolio, it can be deadly serious. Want an example? Let's walk over to the whiteboard again.

Solely market-based financial advisors like to point to **average rate of return** when they are selling you on a particular mutual fund or portfolio grouping. The idea they are putting forth is that it is worth taking a risk because "over time" the gains will outweigh the losses. On the face of it, that sounds fair.

"Look at this prospectus," they will tell you. "Over the last 15 years, the gains average 10%, or 12%, or maybe even 15% (depending on the investment they're promoting)." So let's take a look at this on the whiteboard and see if average rates of return are truly meaningful. Do average rates of return have anything to do with accumulating money?

The first thing we have to remember is that to come up with the average rate of return, we simply have to add up the return for each year, both positive and negative, then divide by the number of years. Simple.

If in year one you have $100 and that $100 **increased** by 100%, how much would you have at the end of that year? Answer: $200.

If in the next year that $200 **decreased** by 60%, how much do you have in actual money? Answer: $80. Now, what is your average rate of return for those two years. Answer: 20%. How did you get that answer? You took the returns of each year, positive and negative, and added them together [+100% and -60% which equals 40%], and then you divided by the number of years involved [two], and that gives you your average rate of return [+20%]. But here's where the smoke and mirrors come in. Did you actually get a 20% return on your money? No. You ended up **losing** 20%. Your $100 is now down to $80. You can't spend average rates of return. You can only spend money. So the average rate of return may have been 20% but the **actual** rate of return was a negative 10%.

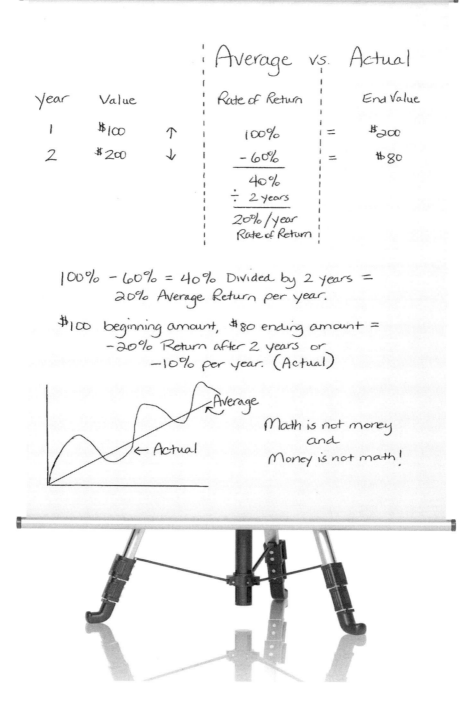

Average vs. Actual

Year	Value		Rate of Return		End Value
1	$100	↑	100%	=	$200
2	$200	↓	− 60%	=	$80

40%
÷ 2 years
20% / year
Rate of Return

100% − 60% = 40% Divided by 2 years =
20% Average Return per year.

$100 beginning amount, $80 ending amount =
−20% Return after 2 years or
−10% per year. (Actual)

Average

← Actual

Math is not money
and
Money is not math!

Remember, math is not money and money is not math! You can't use averages when you are talking about returns on your investments because as soon as you get a negative number, it skews the data.

Let's look at this example as if it were a real portfolio.

If someone had $100,000 and in year one it increased by 10%, in year two it decreased by 10%, and so on throughout 10 years, to where you had five years of 10% increases and five years of 10% decreases, how much would you have in your account? Some will not hesitate to say, $100,000!

"You had as many ups and you did downs, so it leveled out," they may say. "You should have what you started with, shouldn't you?"

But that's where math is not money and money is not math. Fifty minus 50 is zero, divided by 10 years, is a 0% rate of return. But if you do the *actual* instead of the *average,* you take $100,000, add 10% to it and you have $110,000. Everything that happens after that must take into account that changed amount. For example, if you take away 10% from this new amount, $110,000, you are taking away a greater portion than from the original number of $100,000. You are taking away $11,000. So now you are down to $99,000. So the returns of any given account may *average* this or that, but the *timing* of those returns is involved. *When* those increases or decreases occurred has a big part to play on how those numbers affected the value of the account. In the above illustration, using $100,000 with five increases of 10% and five decreases of 10% over a 10-year span, you ended up with $95,099 in your account.

So if someone is attempting to laud the virtues of an investment by giving you the *average* rate of return, be careful not to become a victim of that little mathematical shell game. It is very simple to look at the balance sheet of an actual account that experienced those "average" returns and figure the *actual* return of the investment. That's why we use the expression a lot at our office, "It's the return *of* your money that you are interested in, not the return *on* your money." It may seem like a play on words at first, but once you understand it, it makes a lot of sense.

Chapter Twelve

Doing Away With the Downside

As long as you're still working, delaying Social Security benefits probably won't be difficult. If you're able to live on your earned income, why take smaller-than-maximum retirement checks?

What's more, as long as you're working you should be investing in order to build up your retirement. At the time this book was written, Social Security was paying no more than $30,000 a year. You'll need more – probably a lot more – if you want to enjoy a comfortable retirement. The first place many turn in an effort to bolster their savings is the stock market. But investing can be difficult in times when the market is unstable. Stocks have been risky, as we've seen in recent years. Bonds and bank accounts have low yields today, with little indication that yields will move higher soon.

Fortunately, there is one little-known investment you should consider. We will call it a Guaranteed Lifetime Investment and it is offered by many insurance companies and other financial firms. These Guaranteed Lifetime Investments can provide you with substantial returns with little or no downside risk, and they're also tax-deferred. In other words, you won't owe any tax as long as you simply hold onto the investment contract. You'll pay tax when you take withdrawals.

The Guaranteed Lifetime Investment links your returns to the performance of a specific investment index. Some of those indexes track large-company U.S. stocks, such as the S&P 500 and the Dow Jones Industrial Average. Guaranteed Lifetime Investments also might be linked to the Nasdaq 100 (large tech stocks), the S&P Midcap 400 (medium-sized companies), Russell 2000 (small companies) or the EURO STOXX 50. It's important to understand that these investments are **linked** to the stock market through these indices but they are not *invested* in those indices or the individual stocks that they track.

Let's say, for example, that you invest in a Guaranteed Lifetime Investment that is linked to the S&P 500, a common benchmark for the broad U.S. stock market. Terms may vary with this investment, but let's say the balance of the investment account goes up with the value of the index to which it is linked on a one-to-one ratio. In other words, if the index goes up 5%, then so does the account balance. If the index goes up 8% next year, then your investment's account value would go up by 8% as well. Looking pretty good so far, right?

But what if the market goes down? We have learned, some of us the hard way, that stocks can lose value overnight. What happens if the S&P 500 falls by 5% one year? What if it really goes south and loses 20%? How about 40%? The "guaranteed" part of the Guaranteed Lifetime Investment means that your account will not lose. It won't gain. But it won't lose. With this particular investment, zero is your hero in a bad market year. Your gains are locked in at the end of each year. Your account sits on the sidelines and waits for the market to rebound and your growth continues to track the upsides, but never the downsides, of the market. Still looking pretty good? There's more.

The other part of the "guarantee" in these Guaranteed Lifetime Investments is that with some of these investments you are guaranteed a modest minimum return on your account...even in a down year. You stand to receive a substantial upside gain with little or no possibility of loss.

So what's the catch? Guaranteed Lifetime Investments generally have a cap on the upside. In other words, if you want a contract that gives you a no-loss guarantee you might have to settle for, say a 7.3% cap. In that case, if the market sky-rockets one year and gains 25%, your account would rise in value by only 7.3%.

Is this type of tradeoff worthwhile? Does it pay to limit losses if you must also give up the full benefits of a raging bull market? The numbers say yes. For starters, say you invested directly in the S&P 500 index at the end of 1991. Each year since then, you would have enjoyed or suffered a return equal to the change in the index value. In 1995, you would have had a 34.11% return. In 2008, you would have lost 39.23%.

The Value of $1,000 in the S&P 500 from 12/31/1991 through 12/31/2011

Year	End of year close S&P 500	Annual Return	Value of $1,000	1.5% Management Fee
1991	417.09	NA	$1,000	$1,000
1992	435.71	4.46	1044.64	1028.97
1993	466.45	7.06	1118.34	1085.05
1994	459.27	-1.54	1101.13	1052.32
1995	615.93	34.11	1476.73	1390.10
1996	740.74	20.26	1775.97	1646.71
1997	970.43	31.01	2326.67	2124.97
1998	1229.23	26.67	2947.16	2651.29
1999	1469.25	19.53	3522.62	3121.45
2000	1320.28	-10.14	3165.46	2762.88
2001	1148.08	-13.04	2752.60	2366.49
2002	879.82	-23.37	2109.42	1786.33
2003	1111.92	26.38	2665.90	2223.71
2004	1211.92	8.99	2905.66	2387.34
2005	1248.29	3.00	2992.86	2422.10
2006	1418.30	13.62	3400.47	2710.70
2007	1486.36	4.80	3563.64	2798.17
2008	903.25	-39.23	2165.60	1674.92
2009	1115.10	23.45	2673.52	2036.74
2010	1257.64	12.78	3015.27	2262.64
2011	1257.60	0.00	3015.18	2228.63
		148.81		
		Average Rate of Return	Actual Rate of Return	Actual Rate of Return
	148.81 / 20 =	7.44%	5.67%	4.09%

After all the ups and downs, you'd have an annualized return of 5.67% a year. Assuming you would have paid brokerage fees of 1.5% per year, your actual return would have been around 4%. The 20-year period illustrated by the accompanying chart included one of the greatest bull markets of all time, from 1995 through 1999. Throw in the two ferocious bear markets, however, and things level out dramatically. In fact, if you look at just the last 10 years, your annualized return from the S&P 500 would have been negative after fees, you would have lost money!

The Value of $1,000 in the S&P 500 from 12/31/2001 through 12/31/2011

Year	End of year close S&P 500	Annual Return	Value of $1,000	1.5% Management Fee
2001	1148.08	NA	$1,000	$1,000
2002	879.82	-23.37	766.34	754.85
2003	1111.92	26.38	968.50	939.67
2004	1211.92	8.99	1055.61	1008.81
2005	1248.29	3.00	1087.28	1023.50
2006	1418.30	13.62	1235.37	1145.45
2007	1486.36	4.80	1294.65	1182.41
2008	903.25	-39.23	786.75	707.77
2009	1115.10	23.45	971.27	860.66
2010	1257.64	12.78	1095.43	956.12
2011	1257.60	0.00	1095.39	941.74
		30.43		
		Average Rate of Return	Actual Rate of Return	Actual Rate of Return
	30.43 / 10 =	3.04%	0.92%	-0.60%

Now let's see what would have happened if you had been able to buy a Guaranteed Lifetime Investment at the end of 1991. Assume the account was linked to the S&P 500 with a cap of 7.3%, and a guarantee against loss.

To illustrate this, we re-ran the numbers for the past 20 years, substituting 7.3% for any annual return over that amount and 0% for any loss year.

The Value of $1,000 in the S&P 500 from 12/31/1991 through 12/31/2011 NO Negatives 7.30% Cap

Year	End of year close S&P 500	Annual Return	NO Negatives 7.30% Cap	Value of $1,000
1991	417.09	NA		$1,000
1992	435.71	4.46	4.46	1044.60
1993	466.45	7.06	7.06	1118.35
1994	459.27	-1.54	0.00	1118.35
1995	615.93	34.11	7.30	1199.99
1996	740.74	20.26	7.30	1287.59
1997	970.43	31.01	7.30	1381.58
1998	1229.23	26.67	7.30	1482.44
1999	1469.25	19.53	7.30	1590.65
2000	1320.28	-10.14	0.00	1590.65
2001	1148.08	-13.04	0.00	1590.65
2002	879.82	-23.37	0.00	1590.65
2003	1111.92	26.38	7.30	1706.77
2004	1211.92	8.99	7.30	1831.37
2005	1248.29	3.00	3.00	1886.31
2006	1418.30	13.62	7.30	2024.01
2007	1486.36	4.80	4.80	2121.16
2008	903.25	-39.23	0.00	2121.16
2009	1115.10	23.45	7.30	2276.01
2010	1257.64	12.78	7.30	2442.15
2011	1257.60	0.00	0.00	2442.15
		148.81		
			Actual ROR minus	20 Year Actual ROR
	Average Rate of Return	Actual Rate of Return	1.5% Management Fee	NO Negatives 7.30% Cap
	148.81 / 20 = 7.44%	5.67%	4.09%	4.57%

Now you can see the annualized return would have been nearly 4.6% with the Guaranteed Lifetime Investment. Even if you look at the past 10 years, when an investor would have lost money in the S&P 500, the GLI would have returned about 4.4% per year. What's more, our hypothetical guaranteed lifetime investment is tax-deferred, increasing its advantage over taxable, non-guaranteed exposure to the S&P 500.

The Value of $1,000 in the S&P 500 from 12/31/2001 through 12/31/2011 NO Negatives 7.30% Cap

Year	End of year close S&P 500	Annual Return	NO Negatives 7.30% Cap	Value of $1,000
2001	1148.08	NA	NA	1000
2002	879.82	-23.37	0.00	1000.00
2003	1111.92	26.38	7.30	1073.00
2004	1211.92	8.99	7.30	1151.33
2005	1248.29	3.00	3.00	1185.87
2006	1418.30	13.62	7.30	1272.44
2007	1486.36	4.80	4.80	1333.51
2008	903.25	-39.23	0.00	1333.51
2009	1115.10	23.45	7.30	1430.86
2010	1257.64	12.78	7.30	1535.31
2011	1257.60	0.00	0.00	1535.31
		30.43		
			Actual ROR minus	10 Year Actual ROR
	Average Rate of Return	Actual Rate of Return	1.5% Management Fee	NO Negatives 7.30% Cap
	30.43 / 10 = 3.04%	0.92%	-0.60%	4.38%

Never going backwards is huge! Once you lose 20% in a bear market, you need a 25% gain just to break even. Once you lose 50%, you need a 100% gain to get back to even. So an investment vehicle that allows you to avoid huge losses while still participating in the gains can be a real winner, even if you relinquish some potential gains during those bull market stampedes.

Keep in mind that Guaranteed Lifetime Investments are always tax-deferred; at some point the deferred income tax will have to be paid. That's not the case with guaranteed legacy investments. In most cases, death benefits are paid to the beneficiary or beneficiaries you named, and that payout is not subject to income tax. In addition, guaranteed legacy investments may come with better terms than guaranteed lifetime investments – a 14% annual cap instead of 7.3%, perhaps, with a 3% minimum annual return.

So what do you think? On a scale of 1-10 – one being "what a lousy way to invest!" and 10 being "Fantastic! How do I get into this?" – how would you rate the Guaranteed Lifetime Investment?

I ask the question to make a point with you about bias and prejudice. I once did an experiment and described the Guaranteed Lifetime Investment (which, by the way, is not its real name) to a roomful of people at an investment workshop. I told them how it worked, just as it is described in the paragraphs above...how they could not lose their principle, and how their investment would go up when the market rose and that the gains would be locked in when the market fell. I told them about all of the guarantees in place to protect their investment. Then I asked the question: "How many would like to be in that type of investment?" Every hand went up. Overwhelmingly, the group said they found that type of investment appealing. Then I asked, "How many people here like annuities?" Only three hands went up. Then I told them that the investment I had just described, and the one that they had unanimously endorsed was in actuality... (drum roll, please) a **Fixed Indexed Annuity**. So it makes you wonder, then, doesn't it...why annuities get such a bad rap.

Why the Negativity?

As you can see, annuities are a useful, and in some cases a downright necessary, piece of the income planning puzzle. In fact the GAO (Government Accountability Office) even recommends them, saying in one recent report that Americans can "avoid the risk of outliving their assets by saving more, working longer, investing wisely, *delaying Social Security and buying a life annuity.*" So why do some flinch at the very mention of the word "annuity"? From the informal research I've done, I came to the conclusion that it usually is due to a lack of understanding. They have probably been influenced by what they have heard about *variable* annuities, and they now lump all annuities into the same basket.

If the client's situation is a fit, I will recommend annuities. It is one of the core tools I use in retirement planning. Unfortunately, some clients will leave the office and research annuities on their own, only to come to the conclusion that annuities are *terrible* investments. The problem is, when celebrity analysts criticize *variable* annuities, they often fail to distinguish them from fixed and fixed indexed annuities. Suze Orman, AARP, Jane Bryant Quinn and John Biggs all hate *variable* annuities for reasons we will discuss later. But when they omit the word *"variable"* in their rants, or if the viewer simply doesn't hear it, they will often throw the baby out with the bath water and brand all annuities as being alike, when nothing could be further from the truth. I have noticed that some undereducated commentators tend to oversimplify things when discussing any financial strategy that has a few moving parts, which annuities do. Some perfectly sound planning ideas that could really help retiring Americans are left to the mercy of a few quick sound bites. Some media commentators do much disservice to their readers and viewers when they lump all annuities into the same basket and pass on misconceptions. There is as much diversity in annuities as there is in automobiles and sandwiches. It's a little like castigating the Lexus because some consumer had a bad experience with a Yugo.

Is the prejudice toward annuities deserved? Not if you understand the facts. Prejudice is defined as "forming an adverse opinion beforehand, without a true knowledge of the facts." Psychologists tell us that prejudice is human nature. We all have a tendency to judge things before we know them. Have you ever formed an opinion about persons before you really knew them? I thought so. We all do it.

Author David E. Alder, in *Snap Judgment: When to Trust Your Instincts, When to Ignore Them, and How to Avoid Making Big Mistakes with Your Money,* discusses how our instincts and emotions can often harm us when making investment decisions. Here's what he had to say about annuities:

"There are rational reasons to buy an annuity when you retire. The foremost is you don't have to worry about outliving your money. With

a guaranteed check coming in each month, you need never live your final years in poverty. On top of this, annuities also have the potential for higher returns than from traditional investments because of their inbuilt insurance features—if you survive that is. For people who make it into their 90s, the income from an investment in traditional assets would only be 40% compared to the income from the same amount of money spent on an annuity. The fact that people aren't necessarily good at handling their money once they have retired makes the arguments in favor of annuities even more compelling. This is why the wildly enthusiastic consensus among most economists, to say nothing of the insurance industry, is that annuities are a great thing."

Common Misconceptions

Some of the common misconceptions about annuities remind me of the prejudices we establish about certain groups of people. College professors are all absent-minded. Software engineers are bespectacled and wear pocket protectors. Annuities lock up your money.

Liquidity – It is true that annuities are not entirely liquid. It's a trade-off. You exchange a measure of liquidity for guaranteed safety and a guaranteed return on your investment. The idea that annuities are "illiquid" is just plain silly. Yes, there are penalties for early withdrawal, similar to those imposed by banks on certificates of deposits. But most experts think these "surrender charges" are perfectly reasonable and the surrender charge periods are also reasonable. An annuity with a 10-year surrender period is typical. Also typical are surrender charges that start at 12% and go down to zero within those 10 years. Still, there are some critics who point at this and say, "Aha! I told you so!" as if it were some scheme by the insurance company to bilk an unsuspecting public. The criticism is usually from financial advisors who can only sell you stocks and bonds and don't understand the principles of safe-money investing. Surrender fees are there for a reason. If the holder of the annuity pulls his money out early, the insurance company has not had an adequate time to invest the money so as to make a reasonable profit. They are forced to prematurely sell the investments in which they placed your money, thus incurring a loss. The limits the insurance company sets with regard to withdrawals are the foundation for the guarantees they provide. There is a term in the insurance industry, "10-year-walk-away," used to describe the typical annuity. You have no surrender charges after 10 years. You can walk away from the contract if you so desire and do with your money whatever you see fit. Even then, your money isn't locked up. You typically have 10% free withdrawals annually. And by paying the surrender charge, you can close out the account and place your money somewhere else.

Chapter Thirteen

Not All Annuities Are Created Equal

Here is a truth about annuities that is neither self-evident nor widely understood – not all annuities are created equal. In fact, I sometimes wish there was another word for this financial instrument because it misunderstood by so many.

Originally, an annuity simply meant an annual payment. The Latin word for year is *Annus,* from which we get such words as *annual* and *per annum.* In ancient Rome, soldiers were given an annuity, or an annual salary, when they retired from the military. British businessmen developed life expectancy tables in the sixteenth century and came up with contracts that would allow private individuals to create their own annuities, or lifetime yearly payments. Pay a premium to an insurance company now in return for a yearly stipend later on in life. Since then the basic idea of annuities have metamorphosed into financial instruments that perform all manner of functions along that basic theme.

So why is it that when most people hear the word "annuity" they find two pieces of wood and make the sign of the cross, you know...like they did in those old black and white vampire movies? Mainly it's because they don't understand what they are and how they work. The fact is that there are more types of annuities than Baskin-Robbins® has flavors of ice cream. In this chapter we will consider the five basic kinds of annuities:

- Variable
- Immediate

- Fixed
- Indexed
- Hybrid

Variable Annuities

When people come after you with a deadly weapon when they hear you say the word "annuity," it's probably because they are thinking of *variable* annuities. Why? Because variable annuities can lose value. Variable annuities are essentially stock market investments in an insurance wrapper. They go up in value when the stocks go up. When those stocks fall, your account value falls. With variable annuities, for example, you can start out with $100,000, and a month later, have only $80,000 in your account... or less, depending on how your stocks perform. During the stock market crash of 2008, many who had variable annuities learned this lesson the hard way. Because variable annuities are encased in an annuity shell, they contain provisions that only an insurance company can offer. Death benefits, for example. You can protect your investment for your heirs by tacking on a death benefit rider. This means that if your variable annuity lost, say, half of its value because either you or your advisor picked the wrong stocks, the death benefit would ensure that heirs got the original principle. But just so we are clear, let's assume that you have a variable annuity that was once worth $100,000 but is now worth $80,000, but has a $100,000 death benefit. How much can you withdraw from it? $80,000. Can you pull out the $100,000 death benefit? No. You have to die, and then it doesn't go to you; it goes to your heirs. One of the misconceptions people have about variable annuities is that if they have a death benefit, their annuity is immune from the ups and downs of the stock market. Not true.

As with any other annuity, gains accrued are tax-deferred. Taxes will eventually be paid, however, when those gains are withdrawn.

Because variable annuities have sub accounts similar to mutual funds, they also come with fees and expenses that fixed annuities do not have. These charges include administration fees, mortality fees, expense risk fees, income rider fees, extra charges for the optional death benefit. When it's all said and done most variable annuities are going to cost between 4% and 8% per year in fees. There may be cases where a variable annuity fits that one person out of 20, who needs that one special rider. But as a general rule I find it difficult to endorse them, and most of my colleagues who can see the entire financial planning playing field feel the same way.

Immediate Annuities

Here's what happens with an immediate annuity. You put, say, $100,000 into this financial instrument and it starts paying out right away – thus the term, immediate annuity, as opposed to one you pay into over a period of time. The immediate annuity payout can continue for a certain length of time, which is known as "period certain," or it can pay out for the rest of your life. The amount paid out will be determined by the insurance company using life expectancy tables. The payout can be set up so that it comes to you every month, or every year. Using the figure $100,000 for easy math, a 67-year-old male, for example, can expect to be paid $577 per month for the rest of his life. If he lives to be 102, the payments continue. If he dies a year later, though, the insurance company keeps the balance and heirs get nothing. However, immediate annuities also have a guaranteed payout option. You can have an immediate annuity with a five-year payout to the beneficiary or you can choose a 10-year payout to the beneficiary, or even 15 or 20 years. You get the highest payout if you take a lifetime immediate annuity, which is the one that pays you a certain sum of money and if you die, it's finished.

Let's say you are 67-year-old male and you put $500,000 in the lifetime immediate annuity, then that payout would be $34,608 per year, every single year, for as long as you live, or $2,884 per month. The same $500,000 for female age 65 would yield an annual payout of $30,348 per year for the rest of her life, or $2,529 per month. Why is it lower? Because, generally speaking, females live longer than males. So when calculating a lifetime payout, the insurance company takes into consideration your age, sex, how much you deposit and the payout option.

Fixed Annuities

A fixed annuity is just what it sounds like. It's kind of like a CD, or certificate of deposit, only with an insurance company instead of a bank. You put in $100,000, and five years from now, if you're earning, say 3% interest, you will have $115,927.40. There is one significant difference between a fixed annuity and a CD. You pay taxes as you go with a CD...even if you don't withdraw the money, whereas a fixed annuity is tax-deferred. Usually, you will get a higher rate of return with a fixed annuity than you will with a CD. Like CDs, you will pay a penalty for early withdrawal. With fixed annuities this is called a "surrender charge." Surrender charge periods are usually between three and seven years. Once the annuity is past the surrender charge, you can withdraw your principle and any gains penalty free. You will pay taxes at that time on the gains. You may roll it over into another annuity, or leave it in the same one. As with any annuity, the owner may "annuitize," or exchange the balance of the contract for a payout that can either last for a certain number of years, or guaranteed for the life of the annuitant. A more popular option in the last ten years is to opt for an income rider instead of annuitizing. Why? Because when you annuitize and die early, the insurance company keeps the balance of the account. With an income rider, the annuitant still gets a lifetime payout and, should he or she die early, the balance of the accumulation account is passed on to heirs.

Indexed Annuities

Indexed annuities are sometimes called fixed indexed annuities (FIAs), or equity indexed annuities. Whatever the name, they all work the same. The indexed annuity is a type of fixed annuity that provides a minimum rate of interest, just like the traditional fixed annuity. Call it a "floor." But that's not the end of the story. With these annuities, the rate of return over that floor is predicated on the performance of a stock market index usually the Standard and Poor's 500 (S&P 500) index – thus the name, indexed annuities. The insurance company sets a cap ranging between 4% and 8% on this feature, which means that you get a portion of the positive returns of the market, but do not participate on any of the downsides. In other words, if the S&P jumps up 20% in one year, your growth will hit that cap and stop. The caps are a tradeoff for having guarantee of principle. If the index loses 20%, the value of the indexed annuity is not negatively affected. In that year you get a zero rate of return. Zero is your hero, however, because eliminating the negatives enhances overall growth. Different companies have different rules, percentages and structures. Some have participation rates, some do not. These annuities are relatively new, having appeared on the scene in the early 2000s. They have become increasingly popular with baby boomers approaching retirement because of the growth potential combined with safety. The moving parts of this annuity have been described as a "ratchet/reset." At the contract's anniversary date, the growth is locked in, and becomes the new high-water mark of the annuity. It is that amount that becomes the new balance and represents the new amount that cannot be lost due to market fluctuation. These annuities grow tax-deferred and can be annuitized, or converted, into income streams of various lengths or a lifetime income stream. The addition of income riders has made annuitizing less attractive.

Depending on the insurance company offering it, indexed annuities can come with a bonus feature, which simply means that the insurance company will add a bonus to the amount you deposit. If the insurance company offers, say, a 7% bonus...then you deposit $100,000...your account value is immediately $107,000. Insurance companies compete with brokerage houses, banks and other insurance companies for your money, and bonuses are offered to attract customers.

Hybrid Annuity

A hybrid annuity is merely an indexed annuity with an income rider attached. They are sometimes called "income annuities." What does it mean? It means if you put $500,000 into this annuity, and let's say the company gives you a bonus of 8%, that means you're starting off with $540,000. That is the actual account value. That same $540,000 is also going to be what is referred to as an "income base." In essence, with a hybrid annuity, you have two accounts running simultaneously. The historical average rate of return for an indexed annuity over time is somewhere in the neighborhood of 6%. But let's assume worst-case scenario and attribute just the 1.25% that is guaranteed. After 10 years, your account balance is at least $611,426.

Simultaneously, as the actual accumulation account is growing, the $540,000 income base grows as well, rolling up at, say 7% per year. Again, this varies from company to company, but the idea is the same. If you had $540,000 to work with, that income base rolls up at 7% per year. So at the end of 10 years, in the income base account, your 500,000 is now $1,062,262. If, at that point, you want to turn on that income rider, you may do so. What do you receive in the way of income? Based on the age of 75, a single lifetime payout of 6.5%, or $69,047 per year, every single year, no matter how long you live, for the rest of your life.

So let's extrapolate that. If you get $69,047 per year for 20 years, you would've collected $1,380,940. But you only put in $500,000. And what if you die sooner? Let's say a tragic accident occurs and both you and your spouse are killed after having collected only three payments from your lifetime income, you would have collected a total of $207,141. However, your *real* account value, not your *income* base value, at that time, having grown at only the 1.25% guaranteed rate, would be $634,642. So when you subtract what you have taken, from the real account value, there's $427,501 left for the heirs. Why is that important? Because in an immediate annuity, if you put the money in and you got a payout for your life, once you die it's done; your heirs didn't get any money. With the income rider, however, you get the best of both worlds. You get a guaranteed income that you can't outlive and if you pass away, your heirs get the difference between the actual account value and the amount of income you took. This is why I believe that a hybrid annuity is the best annuity for you if you're looking for income you cannot outlive. By using this as an income source, you are likely able to delay taking your Social Security until age 70, which will make that income as high as possible. You have an income that will keep up with inflation and be larger than it would have been had you taken it at age 62, and you reduce your taxes.

Fees and Commissions – Contrary to opinions put forth by those who are not able to offer them, *fixed annuities* and *fixed indexed annuities* charge no fees. The only exception to that rule is the nominal fee (usually less than 1% of the contract value) when a hybrid annuity utilizes a lifetime income rider. Brokers and bankers typically offer *variable* annuities, which, since they are typically invested in mutual funds type investments, do charge fees called "loads." You will pay these fees, as well as the broker or banker's commissions, with variable annuities even if you lose money. By contrast, fixed and fixed indexed annuities have no risk, no fees except for the nominal charge for optional riders, and no commissions that come out of your balance. Any commissions paid to agents are paid by the insurance carriers that produce the product, similar to the way an airline pays a travel agent. Who does the travel agent work for when he books your trip? YOU! Who pays the agent? The airline the agent uses does. You do not. No self-respecting financial advisor would be influenced by products or by commissions. In fact, the fiduciary relationship that binds most financial advisors prohibits them from allowing even the hint of personal gain to enter into recommendations made to clients. And that is how it should be.

Compare Companies Carefully

When selecting annuities, you must remember there are many makes and models out there. As the title of this chapter suggests, not all annuities are the same. Even within the different *families* or *types* of annuities mentioned here, not all annuities are the same. Insurance companies are like any other profit-making enterprise. They provide product offerings that are designed to add value to your financial life. They plug features into these offerings in order to remain competitive in the marketplace. For example, Company A may offer you a 10% bonus just for placing your money with them instead of Company B. Company B may come back with a 12% bonus next year, but may change some other aspect of the contract to balance out the equation so they can continue to make a profit and stay in business. One of the reasons why you need to seek the help of a retirement *specialist* instead of a *generalist* is that the retirement specialist will keep up with all of these changes and be able to sift out all of the changes and determine for you which company is *actually* offering the best product, all things considered. He or she will know which features are "window dressing" and which ones will positively impact your investment.

Below is a "whiteboard" illustration of three companies, all of which offer what appear to be attractive features in their annuity contracts. Just to make the math easy, we are going to say we have $100,000 to invest. Let's see how we would fare using one over the other two. These are actual companies, by the way. I have just referred to them here as "Company A," "Company B" and "Company C." When you look at their product brochures, you will find features such as these included in the explanation of the products, but unless you understand them, and unless you can see the entire picture, you don't know which is the best. All three companies below offer bonuses. The smallest is 6% and the largest is 8%. In other words, "Do business with us and we will boost the amount you start with right away!" But let's look a little closer.

Company A offers a 6% bonus. Right away, you put $106,000 to work, right? Yes. The bonus is vested 10% per year until it is fully vested. Company A also offers an income rider with a "roll up," that is a guaranteed rate of compounded return of 5% per year for 10 years. Keep in mind this is an income-based account. It is called that, as opposed to the actual "accumulation" account, is because it is actually a calculation base for the eventual lifetime income when you trigger it. So the income base with Company A will grow to $172,663 in 10 years.

Note that all three companies on the whiteboard illustration offer a "payout" rate. Payout rates are determined by age. The older you are, the higher your payout is. So that is one thing to pay attention to. If I am, say 65, what is my "payout rate" on my income rider? These may vary with a percentage point or so from company to company. With Company A, the payout rate for someone 69 years old is 4.5%. If this annuitant decides to trigger his lifetime income stream at age 69, and his income base has grown to $172,663, then his payout is $7,770 per year. Note that Company A offers a *joint life payout.* That is another factor to consider. If you are doing income planning for a couple and the annuity doesn't offer a joint life payout, that is for you and your spouse, it may not be the appropriate choice.

Other things you will learn about Company A's offering as you research it is that it is a *variable* annuity. There's nothing particularly wrong with a variable annuity, but you can lose money in a variable annuity if the market loses money. With a VA, you are invested in sub accounts that invest directly in the stock market. There exist protections in the form of riders, which can be purchased for fees. These riders may prevent your heirs from losing the account base. You can purchase the income rider for a fee, as well, which offers similar protections. But variable annuities can experience loss and can come with exorbitant fees.

Company B blows the doors off the competition with its bonus – a hefty 25%! So, right away, you have $125,000 working for you. A lot of people may pick Company B because the bonus is so big. Company B's income rider rolls up at 5%, just like that of Company A, which means that the income calculation base in 10 years will have grown to $203,612 – more than Company A.

How about the payout? Company B's payout is also 4.5% at age 69, which will give you $9,163 per year, guaranteed for life. But notice that the payout is not *joint* but *single.* Just another factor to consider when doing retirement income planning, and a fully trained professional will spot that difference and point it out if it makes a difference to the client.

The product offering of Company B is a Fixed Index Annuity. FIAs are not subject to market losses because the gains are predicated on the performance of a market index without requiring that the funds be actually invested in the market.

Company C also offers an FIA with an 8% bonus. Right away, you have $108,000 at work. The income rider with Company C's product offering rolls up at a hefty 7% compounded for 10 years. That means the base from which your lifetime income is calculated starts at $212,452. The payout with Company C's annuity is at 5.4%, which means that, once initiated, your lifetime income, for both you and your spouse, will be $11,472. That's a 47.64% increase over Company A and a 25.20% increase over Company B.

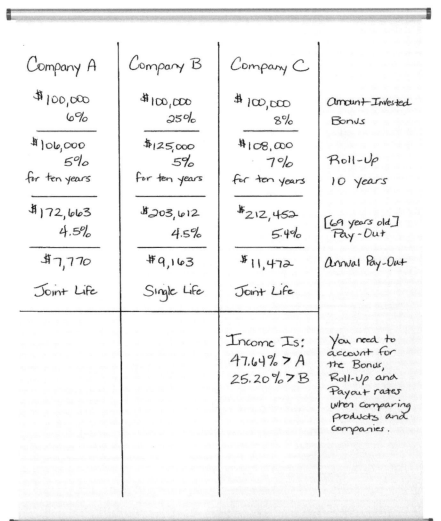

Company A	Company B	Company C	
$100,000	$100,000	$100,000	Amount Invested
6%	25%	8%	Bonus
$106,000	$125,000	$108,000	Roll-Up
5%	5%	7%	
for ten years	for ten years	for ten years	10 years
$172,663	$203,612	$212,452	[69 years old]
4.5%	4.5%	5.4%	Pay-Out
$7,770	$9,163	$11,472	Annual Pay-Out
Joint Life	Single Life	Joint Life	
		Income Is:	You need to account for the Bonus, Roll-Up and Payout rates when comparing products and companies.
		47.64% > A	
		25.20% > B	

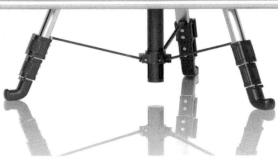

The point is, annuities vary greatly from one to another. It is yet another reason to consult a specialist instead of a generalist when working with these financial instruments. The inside of a watch is complex to the untrained eye, but to a jeweler, it is not. When examining the features of annuities, you need to account for the **bonus,** the **roll-up** and the **payout rates.** You can't just look at just the bonus, or just the roll-up, or just the payout rate by itself. One company may have, say, a 14% **simple interest** roll-up for 10 years. That looks quite attractive. But they don't have a bonus and the payout is only 2.65%. If you chose that product you would have significantly less income. When planning income for life in retirement, the income is, after all, the "bottom line."

Chapter Fourteen

How Safe Are Annuities?

Historians are still debating whether the bank failures of the 1930s caused the Great Depression, or whether the Great Depression caused the bank failures. What is certain is that by 1933, 11,000 of the nation's 25,000 banks failed and closed their doors, leaving many depositors high and dry.

When the public began to learn of the stock market crash of 1929, they began lining up at the teller window to withdraw their money. With no money to lend, and outstanding loans going into default, the banks just couldn't survive.

When Franklin D. Roosevelt became president in 1933, one of his first priorities was to fix the banks. He declared a three-day bank holiday to stop the run on the banks. That stopped the bleeding and probably saved around 1,000 banks. Then, in 1933, the Federal Deposit Insurance Corporation (FDIC) came into being. Even though banks have failed since then, the insurance program worked and depositors were protected. After the stock market crash of 2008, FDIC insured bank accounts upped the limit of insurance from $100,000 per account to $250,000.

But that's banks. What about annuities? Are they FDIC insured? No. Yet, proponents of annuities endorse them as "safe-money" investments in which you cannot lose your principal once you deposit your money unless you withdraw your money prematurely. How is that the case?

Actually, there are more layers of protection for money in an annuity than there are in banks. First of all, you have the assets of the insurance company itself backing up your investment. Insurance companies are some of the most highly regulated companies in America. They are subject to strict capital reserve requirements that are much higher than the capital reserve requirements for banks. Insurance companies (the only entities through which you can purchase an annuity) are required by law to keep at least a dollar in an untouchable reserve account for every dollar of depositors' money they have at risk.

Reinsurance adds another layer of security. In essence, reinsurance is when insurance companies buy insurance. It is insurance that the primary insurer (one that issues policies directly to the public) buys to ensure it has sufficient funding to pay expected claims that may be incurred during the policy period. One way the primary insurer can meet the statutory requirements, other than by having all capital and reserves in cash or cash equivalents, is through a reinsurance structure approved by the financial authorities of the state insurance regulator. Also, insurance companies own corporate bonds that are considered "same as cash" when it comes to safety. The corporations whose bonds they hold are some of the largest and safest corporations in the world. These bonds make regular interest payments to the insurance companies who hold them. Insurance companies also purchase some of the most highly-rated conservative investments available. A large percentage of the capital of these carriers is placed in U.S. *government* bonds, which are, of course, backed by the full faith and credit of the United States government.

A much smaller portion of the assets of insurance companies is placed in conservative A-rated investment real estate, such as large office buildings occupied by Fortune 500 companies. Have you ever noticed that when you drive through a major U.S. city, many skyscrapers and glass towers are insurance buildings? Often these properties are fully paid for, which serves to add to an insurance company's financial security.

Strong Reserves: Which would you say have the strongest reserves, banks or insurance companies? Insurance companies. This is one of the reasons why insurance companies are actually safer than banks and why there have been many more bank failures in America than there have been failures of insurance companies. Example: If a bank takes in $10 million in deposits, it might make $90 million in loans. If only $10 million of those loans default, the bank could exhaust its reserves. When real estate bubbles burst, banks suffer losses on their loans backed up by property values, forcing them to rely on government bailouts where tax-payers' money has to be used to keep them solvent.

Remember when mega-banks like Bear Stearns and Lehman Brothers were in the news because their financial foundations were threatened and they called for government bailouts? According to the October 2011 newsletter posted by annuity brokers WaterStates Financial, multi-billion dollar investment banks use "leverage ratios" of 30 – 1, and even 40 – 1. "In other words, they will speculate with $300 million when they only have $10 million in reserves," says one WaterStates blog. "All it takes is a pronounced market reversal to put a large institution such as that on its ear, which is exactly what happened in the market melt-down of 2008." Insurance companies aren't able to speculate like that.

Wait a minute! What about AIG? Wasn't it part of that melt-down too? Yes. AIG stands for American International Group, not American *Insurance* Group as many surmised. While AIG, the giant insurance conglomerate, overinvested in real estate and mortgages in the years prior to 2008, AIG the insurance company that was a very small part of its parent, AIG the conglomerate, was never in trouble. Even though AIG, the giant insurance conglomerate, had to be bailed out by the federal government after the crash of 2008, the insurance operations were always solvent and stood on their own.

Can an Insurance Company Fail?

Is it possible for an insurance company to go belly-up? Yes. It rarely happens, but insurance companies, if they make bad investments with the profits held outside their reserves, can fail. The bankruptcy of Conseco in 2002 is a good example. So what happens then? If an insurance company does fail, then state guaranty associations guarantee your investment up to a maximum amount. The existence of state guaranty associations should not be a factor in selecting an annuity, but you need to know about them. Each state has rules administered by its department of insurance that requires insurance companies to belong to the guaranty association. If an insurance company fails, policy holders are unharmed because another company steps in and buys that block of business. It's just another layer of protection.

In October 2008, shortly after the market crash and at a time when the nation was jittery over what financial tower would next collapse, *Time* magazine's business and money section ran an article entitled "How Safe Is Your Insurance Company." Here's an excerpt:

"Unlike the banks that have collapsed or merged under pressure, insurance companies are tightly regulated, mostly by the states. The companies are required to keep vast sums of cash and short term investments to be able to pay off policies, and they are required to pay into state funds to protect policy holders in case one of the companies should ever fail."

Chapter Fifteen

Sequence of Returns

Just as a physical setback affects you more dramatically as you age, losses to your retirement savings impact you more significantly when you enter retirement. Time was on your side when you were in your younger years and in the accumulation stage of your life. You were able to take advantage of both the ups and downs of the market. Dollar cost averaging was your friend. But now the rules of the game have changed. You are preparing to take cash out of your nest egg with the same frequency you once put it in, but with a major difference. The amounts are much greater. Market losses right before retirement will not only wipe out years of diligent savings but increase the risk you will run out of savings during retirement and diminish the amount you intended to pass along to your heirs.

There is something called "sequence of returns" that you need to understand. It all has to do with timing. Consider the case of John and Susan. Each one starts out with an account worth $500,000 invested in the stock market. At age 65, they begin taking annual withdrawals of 5% per year. They increase their withdrawals each year by 3% to compensate for inflation. Both accounts earn an average of 8.03%. Both accounts experience three consecutive years of losses.

John

Age	Hypothetical stock market gains or losses	Withdrawal at start of year	Nest Egg at start of year
64			$500,000
65	-10.14%	$25,000	$500,000
66	-13.04%	$25,750	$426,839
67	-23.37%	$26,523	$348,776
68	14.62%	$27,318	$246,956
69	2.03%	$28,138	$251,750
70	12.40%	$28,982	$228,145
71	27.25%	$29,851	$223,862
72	-6.56%	$30,747	$246,879
73	26.31%	$31,669	$201,956
74	4.46%	$32,619	$215,084
75	7.06%	$33,598	$190,610
76	-1.54%	$34,606	$168,090
77	34.11%	$35,644	$131,429
78	20.25%	$36,713	$128,458
79	31.01%	$37,815	$110,335
80	26.67%	$38,949	$95,008
81	19.53%	$40,118	$71,009
82	26.38%	$36,923	$36,923
83	-38.49%	$0	$0
84	3.00%		
85	13.62%		
86	3.53%		
87	26.38%		
88	23.45%		
89	12.78%		

Average return 8.03%	Total withdrawal $580,963

Susan

Age	Hypothetical stock market gains or losses	Withdrawal at start of year	Nest Egg at start of year
64			$500,000
65	12.78%	$25,000	$500,000
66	23.45%	$25,750	$535,716
67	26.38%	$26,523	$629,575
68	3.53%	$27,318	$762,140
69	13.62%	$28,138	$760,755
70	3.00%	$28,982	$832,396
71	-38.49%	$29,851	$827,524
72	26.38%	$30,747	$490,684
73	19.53%	$31,669	$581,270
74	26.67%	$32,619	$656,916
75	31.01%	$33,598	$790,788
76	20.26%	$34,606	$991,981
77	34.11%	$35,644	$1,151,375
78	-1.54	$36,713	$1,496,314
79	7.06%	$37,815	$1,437,133
80	4.46%	$38,949	$1,498,042
81	26.31%	$40,118	$1,524,231
82	-6.56%	$41,321	$1,874,535
83	27.25%	$42,561	$1,712,970
84	12.40%	$43,838	$2,125,604
85	2.03%	$45,153	$2,339,923
86	14.62%	$46.507	$2,341,297
87	-10.14%	$47,903	$2,630,297
88	-13.04%	$49,340	$1,978,993
89	-23.37%	$50,820	$1,677,975

Average return 8.03%	Total withdrawal $911,482

http://www.foxbusiness.com/personal-finance/2012/04/30/solving-myth-rate-return/

At this point, you may think that these two cases are identical but they are not. Why? Because of the timing involved. The three consecutive years of losses happened at *different times* with vastly different results. John took his losses between the ages of 65 and 67, and Susan's account went backwards between ages 87 and 89. Who ran out of money first? John or Susan? Before you answer, consider this important point about "sequence of returns." Market losses just before you retire, or just as you begin your retirement, have a much more negative effect on your retirement account than market losses when you are older. You're right. John ran out of money first.

How were John and Susan affected by the Sequence of Returns? By age 68, after three straight years of market losses, plus the withdrawals, John's $500,000 account had shrunk to around $250,000. Susan's account, however, was up over $750,000 when she was 68...and by the time she was 86, her account was over $2 million. Then three years of losses took it down to around $1.5 million at age 89. John's account never quite recovered from the losses experienced so early in retirement. He ran out of money at age 83.

If you will notice, all we did was reverse the order (or sequence) of the returns of the market. It's the same 25 years, just in reverse order. All we're saying is that timing is critical. Can you time the market? No. Not unless you have a crystal ball. The solution is to adjust your market risk as you approach retirement so you cannot be affected.

Chapter Sixteen

Let's Talk about *Heir* Power

Prejudicial thinking and misconceptions can sometimes warp our judgment when it comes to investing. This is true when it comes to taking care of our families. A television commercial that got my attention a few years back had the catchphrase, "This isn't your father's Oldsmobile." By the late eighties to mid-nineties, the Oldsmobile brand began to be associated with the stodgy, gas-guzzling behemoths they were in the 1970s, and General Motors wanted to let the world know their newly designed Cutlass Supreme model was just what the new generation needed. In order to re-establish its identity and appeal to a younger audience, the auto maker aired several 15-second spots featuring the perky Cutlass, ending each of them with the line: "This is not your father's Oldsmobile."

Like annuities, life insurance was completely overhauled in the decade that spanned the late 1990s and the early 2000s. What has not been overhauled, however, is public opinion about life insurance and its usefulness when it comes to estate planning and retirement income strategies. If we were to do a word association test, sort of like the psychologists perform, when you say the words "life insurance," most people would say, "complicated," or "death" or "salesman." I seriously doubt if anyone would utter the words "tax-free retirement" or "a way to become my own banker," but again, that's just because of lack of education. The truth is, today's insurance contracts are completely different from those of yesteryear. What comes next *is not* your father's insurance policy.

In the past few years, the capped-upside/guaranteed downside concept has moved from the annuity world to the world of insurance. A more accurate name for this innovative product would be "legacy investment," instead of insurance. But in the industry, it is called an EIUL, or Equity Indexed Universal Life.

The value of these products lies in the fact that they have a cash value–an investment account that can grow over time because it is linked to the growth of the stock market but does not participate in the market's losses. Similar to the indexed annuities, there will be a cap on the upside and guarantees against losses on the downside. Similar to the annuity products, you won't owe any tax as long as you keep the money inside the contract. But because it is a life insurance product, you are entitled to certain extra tax benefits. Any investment income within the cash value won't be taxed at all, and it is possible to even tap the cash value, tax-free, with withdrawals and loans. But tax-free access to this account is permitted as long as you follow the rules of the contract. In contrast, withdrawals from indexed annuity accounts are usually subject to income tax and perhaps a 10% penalty before age 59½. Keep in mind that with tax-deferred fixed indexed annuities, the taxes will have to be paid at some point. That's not the case with EIULs. Death benefits from a life insurance policy are, by law, paid income tax-free. Hence, the EIULs guaranteed legacy investments may come with better terms than can be offered by annuities, namely a higher cap and a higher guaranteed floor. While the actual caps and floors vary from company to company and can be changed year-to-year depending on the prevailing interest rate environment, it is not atypical for EIULs to offer an investment account with a 14% annual cap instead of 7.3% annual cap, and a minimum annual return of 3%.

Consumers who purchase these life insurance policies do so more for the tax-free investment potential than for the death benefit, but the death benefit is certainly there. Simply put, the appeal is cash when you're living and a legacy to your family should you die. These investments, similar to their annuity cousins, track a stock market index, such as the S&P 500. Consider the following example of how

$1,000 placed in one of these financial instruments would grow over an actual 20-year period tracking the S&P 500 from 12/31/1991 through 12/31/2011:

The Value of $1,000 in the S&P 500 from 12/31/1991 through 12/31/2011 NO Negatives 14% Cap

Year	End of year close S&P 500	Annual Return	NO Negatives 14.00% Cap	Value of $1,000
1991	417.09	NA		$1,000
1992	435.71	4.46	4.46	1044.60
1993	466.45	7.06	7.06	1118.35
1994	459.27	-1.54	0.00	1118.35
1995	615.93	34.11	14.00	1274.92
1996	740.74	20.26	14.00	1453.41
1997	970.43	31.01	14.00	1656.88
1998	1229.23	26.67	14.00	1888.85
1999	1469.25	19.53	14.00	2153.29
2000	1320.28	-10.14	0.00	2153.29
2001	1148.08	-13.04	0.00	2153.29
2002	879.82	-23.37	0.00	2153.29
2003	1111.92	26.38	14.00	2454.74
2004	1211.92	8.99	8.99	2675.43
2005	1248.29	3.00	3.00	2755.69
2006	1418.30	13.62	13.62	2024.01
2007	1486.36	4.80	4.80	3131.01
2008	903.25	-39.23	0.00	3281.30
2009	1115.10	23.45	14.00	3740.69
2010	1257.64	12.78	12.78	4218.74
2011	1257.60	0.00	0.00	4218.74
		148.81		
			Actual ROR minus	20 Year Actual ROR
	Last 20 Years Average ROR	20 Year Actual ROR	1.5% Management Fee	NO Negatives 14% Cap
	148.81 / 20 = 7.44%	5.67%	4.09%	7.46%

How would the same strategy work in a shorter time frame? In the following example, an actual 10-year time span is used with returns reflective of the performance of the S&P 500 Index from 12/31/2001 through 12/31/2011.

The Value of $1,000 in the S&P 500 from 12/31/2001 through 12/31/2011 NO Negatives 14% Cap

Year	End of year close S&P 500	Annual Return	NO Negatives 14.00% Cap	Value of $1,000
2001	1148.08	NA	NA	$1000
2002	879.82	-23.37	0.00	1000.00
2003	1111.92	26.38	14.00	1140.00
2004	1211.92	8.99	8.99	1242.49
2005	1248.29	3.00	3.00	1279.76
2006	1418.30	13.62	13.62	1454.06
2007	1486.36	4.80	4.80	1523.86
2008	903.25	-39.23	0.00	1523.86
2009	1115.10	23.45	14.00	1737.20
2010	1257.64	12.78	12.78	1959.21
2011	1257.60	0.00	0.00	1959.21
		30.43		
			Actual ROR minus	10 Year Actual ROR
	Last 10 Years Average ROR	10 Year Actual ROR	1.5% Management Fee	No Negatives 14% Cap
	30.43 / 10 = 3.04%	0.92%	-0.60%	6.96%

Retirement Planning with an EIUL

People over the age of 70½ who have qualified accounts, such as IRAs, often complain when they have to take required minimum distributions from those accounts. One such individual huffed, "I do not need the money. I would prefer to leave it there and let it grow for my grandchildren." We understand how these folks feel, but that's just not the way the IRS plays the game. Uncle Sam knows what he is doing with tax-deferred accounts. You made a deal with him. He said, "Pay me now or pay me later." Later is when you turn 70½ and your RMDs kick in. But here's what some people are now doing if they are healthy enough to qualify: They take those forced withdrawals and use them to pay the premiums on an Equity Indexed Universal Life insurance policy. If they die early, the insurance pays a handsome, tax-free death benefit to their heirs. If they continue to live, they may make regular, tax-free withdrawals from the growth of the policy to supplement their retirement income.

I am not saying that the EIUL approach to retirement planning is always a better way to invest than with fixed indexed annuities. Many factors enter in, not the least of which is the age of the individual and the amount of the EIUL premium. But since the time value of money and the principles of compound interest are at work here, too, time figures into the equation. Indexed annuities are meant to provide retirement income. If you wish, you can take every penny from an FIA and use it for living expenses as you grow older.

Simply put, an EIUL can be an effective choice to provide for your loved ones after your death and to supplement your retirement income. An annuity is an excellent vehicle to create an income you cannot outlive. Both products have a few moving parts, and it is wise to seek help from a knowledgeable investment advisor who can evaluate the attributes of each of these unique offerings and help you determine if they are a fit for your retirement plan. But it is worth considering the value of such a plan since it has upside potential, meaningful guarantees, and does away with the negatives, giving the investor growth without stress.

Chapter Seventeen

The Roth IRA Revolution

Most of my work centers around retirement planning, so needless to say most of my clients are...well, let's put it this way, they are approaching that time in their lives when they start getting subscription offers from the AARP and are likely to qualify for senior discounts. But not all of the people with whom I interact professionally are older. If I have the opportunity to help guide the steps of young people financially, I will tell them, from the heart, that they should (a) live within their means, (b) start saving now for their retirement, if they haven't already begun, and (c) open up a Roth IRA.

"What's a Roth IRA?" they will sometimes ask. I don't roll my eyes, but I feel like it. The schools should be teaching this, I think to myself. Maybe it's because educators think this kind of thing is over the heads of today's youth. But I can't understand how some can finish four years of college and not know something as basic to their financial wellbeing as what a Roth IRA is.

The Roth IRA was named after the late Senator William Roth of Delaware, who was known as a fiscal conservative who hated taxes. He helped engineer the Economic Recovery Tax Act of 1981, also known as the Kemp-Roth Tax Cut. He also led the charge to establish the type of individual retirement account plan that would allow you to pay taxes on the *front end* of an IRA and withdraw it tax-free on the *back end.* Why is that important? Let me illustrate it this way:

Suppose you are a farmer. You go into your local feed and seed store to buy your seed for this year's corn crop. Uncle Sam is there with his top hat. In the hat band of his hat there is a tag that reads, "IRS." That gives you a clue that he is not there to recruit you into the army; he is there to talk to you about taxes.

"Before you buy that seed," he says, "I would like to make you a proposition. You can either pay tax on the seed now and be done with it, or I can let you have the seed tax-free. But when it is harvest time and you reap your crop, I will tax you on the harvest. So what's it going to be?"

"Are you kidding me???" you reply. "I would much rather pay you taxes on the seed and not pay any taxes on the harvest!"

As silly as it sounds, that's exactly what tax deferment amounts to. When we go to work and sink part of our paycheck into a traditional 401(k), for example, we are not paying any income tax on the money contributed. It grows throughout our working years, and then we harvest the money to live on in retirement. We pay taxes on it then.

That arrangement was the only game in town until the Roth IRA became available in 1998. Then in 2006, the other piece of the tax-free retirement account puzzle clicked in – the Roth 401(k) – which is slowly finding its way into corporate America (not all employers offer it yet).

The argument for tax-deferred plans has always been that you build up your account while you're working, and in a higher tax bracket, and tap into it when your income falls and you are ostensibly in a lower tax bracket. There's only one hitch to that thinking. We don't *know* what taxes will be in the future. But with the national debt clock rolling up trillions of future obligations, all indications are that taxes will be higher, not lower, in the future. But if you do your investing in a Roth IRA, you are dealing with a known quantity. Like all IRAs, taxes are a non-issue as long as the money stays within the account. But there is a huge difference between a Roth IRA and a traditional IRA when you take the money out. You must understand that Roth IRAs are always funded with tax dollars, which means that you won't get a tax deduction when you contribute to a Roth. But your distributions will be completely tax-free after you've had the account for five years, and after you reach age 59½.

Suppose you're 40 years old now. Every year you contribute to a Roth IRA. Over the next 20 years, you might contribute a total of $100,000. With earnings, your account could grow to $150,000, $200,000, or more. Then, because you would be older than 59½, you could take out as much as you'd like, year after year. Your neighbors might be paying sky-high tax rates on their income by then, while you're pulling tax-free dollars from your Roth IRA.

Indexed Investing

Living in sunny Florida as I do, I have little opportunity to walk on ice of any kind. But from all that I have read, the best way to cross ice thinner than four inches thick is to crawl. Crawling across the ice gives you four points of contact instead of two. Your weight is more evenly distributed and there is much less chance of falling through.

Index investing is the same thing in principle. Investing can be a risky business if you put all your eggs in one basket. Spread them out and you even out that risk. As we have seen in prior chapters, investing via an index within the framework of an fixed index annuity would have beaten the results of having invested directly in the S&P 500 during the past 20 years and would have far outpaced being directly invested in the S&P 500 over the past 10 years. So, if you're looking for a way to invest inside your Roth IRA, where you want a strong long-term performer, fixed indexed annuities can be an excellent choice. You accomplish three things. You protect your assets from downside market risk, participate in long-term stock market growth, and enjoy tax-free distribution of withdrawals. Some FIA contracts allow you to diversify your Roth IRA investments by tracking indices that reflect large-capitalization U.S. companies (large cap), midsize companies (mid-cap) and smaller companies (small-cap). You may also use an index that follows technical stocks, foreign stocks and others that are linked to commodities, gold prices and real estate.

You might hear or read something that challenges this line of approach, like: "Guaranteed lifetime investments don't belong in an

IRA," or "Why would you buy a tax-deferred vehicle such as an annuity and put it inside a tax-deferred account such as an IRA?"

Actually, there is a rationale for putting a tax-deferred annuity inside another tax-deferred account. Fixed indexed annuities can offer protection against account losses, since they are immune to the downside risk of the market, and they allow you to withdraw certain amounts, year after year. You simply don't have those guarantees if you buy common stocks or stock funds for your IRA. Assuming the minimum requirements (five-year holding period, age 59½) are met, a Roth IRA becomes a *tax-free* account. You can invest for decades and eventually extract all the earnings without owing income tax. It simply makes good sense to do as much investing as possible within the shell of a Roth IRA, where your distributions can be tax-free, and invest through an index so your growth will be based on a broader picture of the stock market. It is my opinion that, if you have a Roth IRA, it should be the place of last resort to withdraw money for ordinary living expenses.

Roth IRAs offer yet one more tax advantage. While investors must take at least their required minimum distributions (RMDs) from a traditional IRA, after age 70½, Roth IRA owners aren't required to take RMDs. You can take tax-free withdrawals, if you wish, but if you don't need the money you can leave your Roth IRA to grow for your beneficiaries, who can then take tax-free withdrawals after they inherit the account.

Stretching Your IRA

In my experience as a financial planner, many people know that an Individual Retirement Account can be a powerful way to save for retirement but few are aware of its effectiveness as an estate-planning tool. It is possible to transfer wealth to future generations while at the same time reducing, deferring or even eliminating income taxes on your retirement savings. The strategy of IRA owners pushing the wealth forward to their children and grandchildren is called "stretching" the IRA. The concept helps you extend the account's tax-deferred compounding to your heirs. Anyone who has beneficiaries whom they expect will outlive them (a younger spouse, children, grandchildren) can use this strategy. It is not for everyone. But if you don't need the money in your IRA to make ends meet, then it may be something to consider.

How to Stretch an IRA

The key in stretching an IRA is properly designating your beneficiaries. I am constantly surprised at how little thought some people give to the beneficiaries on their IRAs. Some are not even aware they need to care for this detail. One of the first things a competent financial advisor should do when completing an IRA analysis is to check to see who the designated beneficiary is. On some documents I have seen, the beneficiary line is blank. In other cases where the document has not been updated for several years, the designated beneficiary may be someone who is deceased or a former spouse. If you die, your assets will transfer as you have specified in the IRA document – not according to what's in your will.

Stretching an IRA can be as simple as naming one or more beneficiaries who are younger than you. You take only the required minimum distributions (RMDs) during your lifetime, leaving the remainder to continue growing tax-deferred while you're still alive. Most married IRA owners will name their spouse as primary beneficiary and, if they have children, name the children or grandchildren as secondary beneficiaries. Beneficiaries are usually family members, but they can be friends, a family trust or a charitable organization. But if the goal is to preserve wealth for future generations, a stretch IRA will generally allow you to transfer more money to younger beneficiaries when the primary beneficiary dies before the primary beneficiary depletes the account. This allows the other beneficiaries to inherit what is left in the account.

Stretching the Distributions

When you die, your beneficiaries will have some distribution options. What they choose to do may depend on whether they are spousal or non-spousal beneficiaries and whether or not you began taking your RMDs from the account. Keep in mind, each option will have its own tax consequences that will vary according to individual circumstances. For example, the beneficiary may:

- Take a lump sum
- Transfer the account balance to an inherited IRA with a five-year time limit for starting distributions
- Transfer the account balance to an inherited IRA that distributes assets according to the beneficiary's life expectancy as shown in the IRS life expectancy table.

If you have heard of IRA owners stretching a $1 Million IRA account to $4 million to future generations over time, it is most likely the last option that has been exercised. While the beneficiary is draining the smallest amount possible from the account, the rest of the money is left to grow at compound interest.

Remember, spousal beneficiaries have the additional option of requesting a spousal transfer, which allows them to roll over the account balance into an IRA in his or her own name.

Stretching a Roth IRA

Can you stretch a Roth IRA? Yes. Check with your financial advisor for details as to eligibility and suitability, but stretching a Roth IRA can be even more effective than stretching a traditional IRA. Roth IRA contributions are not tax-deductible, but your investments grow tax-deferred and earnings can be withdrawn income-tax-free if you're at least 59½ and have had the Roth at least five years. One of the best things about the Roth IRA is that there are no RMDs at age 70½. Because of these benefits, using a Roth IRA for your stretch IRA strategy may be a smart choice if you have significant IRA balances that you don't plan to tap during your lifetime. Will the value of a Roth IRA be included in your estate? While the value of a Roth IRA will be included in your estate, the account could grow larger than it otherwise might under traditional IRA distribution rules, potentially leaving more money for your heirs. Another plus is that your beneficiaries will be able to make income-tax-free withdrawals during their lifetimes. The value of this is obvious. It is as if you have prepaid the income tax on their inheritance from your taxable estate by converting traditional IRAs that you did not need into Roth IRAs during your lifetime.

This is a broad brush explanation. Please consult your financial advisor for details as they specifically relate to your estate.

Chapter Eighteen

The Danger of Focusing Exclusively on Accumulation in Retirement Planning

I am not a conspiracy theorist. I do not believe that the recent removal of Twinkies from the grocery shelves was part of a Communist plot. I don't think our own government faked the bombing of the twin towers of the World Trade Center in 2001, and I do believe that, yes, men actually landed on the moon, and no, it wasn't all filmed in the Arizona desert. I suppose it also makes me naïve to say that I believe Lee Harvey Oswald acted alone in the Kennedy assignation. But I do believe there is an ongoing effort by the media and some in the financial community to focus our attention solely on the accumulation of assets instead of the preservation and cautionary use of our assets.

Call me crazy, but I believe that we are purposely being fed unbalanced and dangerous advice from some magazines, market analysts, and some of the talking heads on TV's financial networks. When I tune into a television program dealing with finance or pick up a magazine devoted to the subject of investing, there is little of substance presented that acknowledges the two distinct phases of our economic lives: accumulation and distribution. The media seems to be pushing only the accumulation side. Why is that?

One clue may be to check out who pays the bills. Most of the ads in the magazines come from brokerage houses, which know only one concept of growing your savings for your eventual retirement – putting it at risk in the stock market. Frankly, that's not bad for someone who is in their forties and has years to make up for market losses by capitalizing on subsequent gains. Those investors who are approaching retirement are inundated with information that directs them to the solely market-biased investing philosophies and nary a whisper is heard about safe-money approaches to savings growth.

In their white paper "Accumulation Conditioning of Investors and Advisers," Christine G. Russell and Sean M. Ciemiewicz make the point that major media messages around retirement focus almost exclusively on accumulation, and that it has a conditioning effect. They contend that "both investors and advisers balk at changing tactics to accommodate the *spending* phase of retirement." According to Russell and Ciemiewicz, this conditioning causes "sub-optimal" outcomes for many investors when they begin living in retirement.

Because schools offer little in the way of education on how to handle finances in the adult world, most people pick up bits and pieces here and there as they grope their way along. If you've ever had an employer who sponsored a 401(k) plan, you probably formed many of your opinions about investing from the employee meetings where those savings and investment programs were explained. Perhaps they dealt with asset allocation, diversification, dollar cost averaging and the dangers of taking out loans unnecessarily. But little is ever said about the end game, when you are nearing retirement, or what to do when the paychecks stop and it's time to replace them with your savings – the spending phase, in other words.

What happens when those approaching retirement reach out to acquire an education? The deck seems stacked against them. Most advice sources seem to speak only the language of accumulation, not preservation and distribution. Decisions at this stage of the game are more critical too. An investing mistake made early on in life can be lived through and overcome because time is on your side. More money is involved in investment decisions made toward the end of our working years and into retirement. A $1,000 error is much easier to compensate for than a $100,000 error.

Russell and Ciemiewicz also believe that seniors, like it or not, are at a cognitive disadvantage. They contend that we peak in middle age when it comes to our ability to make financial decisions. Couple that with the fact that all these retirees have ever heard about handling their finances tends to revolve around accumulation, and not with what to do with what they have accumulated when it is time to retire. Naturally, their decisions are going to reflect that. At just the time in their lives when they need to obtain and process new information on the spending phase of their lives, they experience a decline in both their ability and their willingness to do so.

Russell and Ciemiewicz also zeroed in on the root cause for many poor decisions made by retirees – reluctance to seek professional help. They quote a survey done by the MetLife Mature Market Institute revealing that only 49% of retirement decisions were made using the advice of a financial planner. Most were by people who trusted their own judgment and instincts. This doesn't surprise me. The financial advisory community appears to be divided on many issues. There seems to be a continental divide of sorts between those who would have every dollar and dime of a retiree's money invested in risk-bearing investments and those who would insist that no investment risk whatsoever should be taken by anyone over 60. As is the case with many dichotomies of thought, the truth is in the middle.

Advice seekers are confused, however, and many tend to ask the advice of a relative, friend, or co-worker before making a financial decision. Why? Because they feel they can trust them and that their relative, friend or co-worker has no dog in the hunt, and is apt to give them unbiased advice. In short, the individuals are within their circle of trust, while the financial advisor is not. Understandable! When it comes to your money, trust plays a huge part in determining whom you believe. More than experience. More than expertise. There's an old expression, "Once burned, twice shy." Those who experienced dramatic losses in their retirement portfolios while their advisor sat silently by are less likely to trust so openly again. Can you blame them?

The MetLife study reported that 48% of those who choose to take the do-it-yourself approach to retirement planning spend fewer than 10 hours per year in preparation for the complexities they may face in retirement. Since their "education" to that point in their lives has been accumulation-biased, they are less likely to make informed decisions. The report issued by Russell and Ciemiewicz makes the following observation:

"For instance, perhaps these factors account for the bias against using an annuity that many individuals exhibit. Using an annuity for retirement income can be an effective and extremely useful tool, but when asked, or presented with an annuity option, many investors refuse to invest any of their accumulated retirement savings – even just partially. Even the word, "annuity," can bring forth a bias against using this product. Excuses for not using an annuity include: 'I have heard they are bad;' 'A certain TV personality said they are not a good investment option,' 'They have high fees so they are not good for me,' 'I don't want to tie up my money for a long time,' and 'I can't get my money out.' While options and benefits surrounding various annuity types can be appealing to an individual for a portion of their assets, they often change their mind and reject the idea merely because the "annuity" word is used. What amounts to a clear cost/benefit analysis turns into a preconceived opinion that annuities are bad. It seems plausible that this bias was either magnified or created by conditioning. While an annuity may not be appropriate in all instances, some annuities may help solve critical issues for retirees."

Earlier in this book I referred to the Wharton School, University of Pennsylvania, one of the most prestigious business schools in America. Their research in all things pertaining to investment and retirement planning is done by professors who have no merchandise to push, no advertisers to please and no agenda to promote. In other words, it is unbiased. Their research is quite comprehensive and is available to anyone free of charge. I'm not going to tell you their recent report on Real World Index Annuity Returns is a good book for the beach, nor is Professor David Babbel, who compiled the work, the next Stephen King. But if you want an unbiased, factual and statistical education, it's worth the read.

Sadly, many Americans these days get their financial education from TV program sound bites. I know some individuals who rely on the unrestrained antics of a stock picker on one of the ubiquitous money and investment networks. He comes out ringing a cow bell, yelling at the camera and honking a bulb horn for comedic effect. He's been wrong as much as he has been right about his predictions, but hey... he's on TV, so he must know what he's doing, right?

The truth is, these cable and satellite television shows condition investors, not on prudent retirement strategies, but on accumulation strategy. The messages they contain are often carefully designed to appeal to as many investors as possible and focus on the excitement of "beating the odds" by picking the winners and dumping the losers, as these show hosts perceive them to be. Focused more on hype and ratings, they will put the spotlight on what is sexy, not on the boringly conservative "decumulation" end of the spectrum. What drops out the bottom is an ill-informed, unprepared and often mis-invested retiring public that simply doesn't know what it doesn't know, which is the worst kind of ignorance one can possess.

The Russell and Ciemiewicz report concludes:

"Accumulation of assets works very well during the working and prime saving years of investors, but during one's retirement, products used and strategies employed must change. Failing such a change, the investor may run out of money too soon, or spend too little in retirement. Thus, investors deprive themselves during the final phase of their lives. Even with all the emphasis on accumulation, investors still make many questionable planning decisions."

What the Future Holds

Those who know me know that I am a glass-half-full kind of guy. I believe that, as an industry, financial advisory firms are becoming more educated as the baby boomers age and approach retirement at the rate of 10,000 per day. This group has demanded change all their lives and have gotten it. When something doesn't make fiscal sense to them, boomers don't tolerate it for very long before they put economic pressure on the marketplace for change. That's why the insurance industry revamped their annuities a decade ago. That's why we see alternative ways of providing long-term care. This same spirit will also, in my opinion, force advisors who have blinders on to see the light and show that they understand the complexity of retirement-income planning.

I believe experiences like the last market crash in 2008 will be a positive for retiring investors of the boom generation. The hue and cry for more guarantees, less risk and preservation-oriented strategies for retirement will not be stifled. Many advisors who have been looking down Wall Street and now starting to look down Main Street and are beginning to better educate their retiree clients in investing concepts that fit their stage of life and not simply going to the same well for solutions that no longer work.

There is an old expression, "nature abhors a vacuum." Well, so does free enterprise. Necessity is often the mother of invention in the world of business and finance. We have yet to see many of the positive changes that will take place to make investing ones' money a safer endeavor. Independent advisors with fiduciary duty to their clients, and not to any one organization, will be the first ones to catch that wave and help their clients benefit from the new direction. I read recently an interesting article by Stanford University Fellow Vivek Wadhwa, who pointed out that one of the great concerns of the world, clean water, may see a solution through the enterprising efforts of the man who invented the Segway personal transporter, which is a one-person scooter becoming popular in airports and malls.

Dean Kamen calls his new device that he anticipates will keep countries such as India, China and parts of the Middle East from running out of water in this century, the "Slingshot." It's a vapor-compression water-purification machine that can produce about 30 liters of 100% pure distilled water per hour using the same power as a hair dryer consumes. It can transform dirty water from any source: rivers, oceans and even raw sewage. According to Wadhwa, Slingshot was recently tested by the Coca-Cola® Company for six months in Africa and the device worked flawlessly. Desalinating water has been going on for decades, but the energy required makes it too expensive for the masses. This way, problem solved. Millions of lives saved.

Disease and sickness from water-borne viruses and bacteria eliminated. As more and more retirees flood the socio-economic scene, the tone and tune of the media will be forced to change and give them what they need instead of what serves the barons of Wall Street. If we can put men on the moon and we can solve the world's water problems, then we can correct the trend of the media "conditioning" advisors and investors to their detriment.

Chapter Nineteen

The Concept of Acting
as Your Own Bank

Albert Einstein was right to call compound interest the eighth wonder of the world. Like the atom, it can accomplish powerful things. Two things are true about compound interest: It works best (a) over time, and (b) if you leave it alone. The concept of the interest earning interest on interest earning interest is the simple reason why the rich get richer. It's an immutable law of finance.

If you stop and think about it, whether we know it or not, we finance everything we buy. "But wait a minute," you say. "I pay cash for everything I own." Really? The cash you pay could be earning interest if you had kept it, couldn't it? So by forfeiting that potential interest, you essentially financed it, right? If you paid cash, you have to make payments to yourself to get back to where you were before you made the purchase.

The Infinite Banking Concept® is one rapidly growing in popularity among those whose goal is to create wealth for themselves instead of creating more wealth for the lending institutions. The concept was developed by Nelson Nash, who is also the author of *Becoming Your Own Banker.* The intent is to provide foundational financial wisdom that will help consumers understand personal finance and partially recover the interest they needlessly give to financial institutions – *and on a tax-free basis!* Once cash value has been established in a life insurance instrument, such as the one used by the Infinite Banking Concept,® the portion of the interest you pay yourself back is plowed right back into your account and continues to grow compounded.

Once people understand the wealth-building power behind this concept, they sometimes ask why someone didn't come up with the idea sooner. Nash makes the observation that the underlying contract of a whole life dividend paying life insurance policy has not fundamentally changed in over 100 years.

"This contract is central to the entire system," says Nash. "So, the concept of how to convert that contract into a tax-advantaged vehicle with similar transactional mechanics of the banking process is what has been developed."

Nash adds that the Infinite Banking Concept® is not a "get rich quick" concept, but rather a program that requires a commitment of long-term discipline to save. Even Nash acknowledges that it is a major paradigm shift for most folks. It may require a few sessions with a financial professional who is fully trained in the concept and is able to explain it thoroughly. But, once understood, the idea can save the farsighted consumer thousands, if not hundreds of thousands of dollars.

The Private Reserve Strategy™ is another concept that gives us a new way to look at how money works. Developed by insurance industry spokesman and software creator Don Blanton, the strategy is designed to teach people how to avoid what Blanton calls, "unnecessary wealth transfers" where possible and accumulate an increasing pool of capital that you can access and control.

What Type of Account Should You Use?

What type of account should you use for your private reserve strategy? The idea is to use an account that offers you the greatest number of benefits and where your money is available to you through collateralization. Optimally, the account would incorporate the following benefits:

Tax deferred growth. Compounding interest in a taxable account, such as a CD or a regular savings account, is not going to serve you well.

Tax-free distribution. To be able to get the money out without having to pay taxes on it would be awesome!

Competitive rate of return. During the accumulation phase you want the interest to be as high as possible.

High Contributions. Some accounts come with contribution limits. You want to be able to put as much as you wish into the account.

Deductible contributions. This would be highly preferred.

Collateral opportunities. This is key for the private-banker strategy to work. Otherwise, how will you be able to leverage the two accounts?

Safe Harbor. You want the money in the account to be safe.

No-loss provisions. You want to be immune from losses.

Guaranteed loan options. If you are going to collateralize loans from time to time, you're going to be able to do it at your discretion with guaranteed access.

Unstructured loan payments. This would be preferred. You do want to pay the money back, but you are not under any obligation to do so under a set and rigid schedule, thus eliminating the pressure of forced payments.

Liquidity, use and control. You will want liquidity, use and control of the money at all times.

Additional benefits. It would be nice to have your account protected in case of a lawsuit or an attack by creditors.

So where can you find an account like that? You certainly won't find it advertised by your local bank. That would be tantamount to the oil industry advertising solar power.

There are perhaps several accounts that will enable you to leverage compounding interest against an amortized loan, but none that I know of that will provide you with all the attributes listed above in quite the way life insurance will. Before you slam the book shut and attempt to light fire to it, please know that I'm not talking about life insurance as you probably have always thought it to be – a payment to a beneficiary when someone dies. This is a concept that *uses* the tax advantages life insurance enjoys courtesy of Uncle Sam and the IRS, and the cash growth features that only life insurance can legally provide. To fully understand the value of the Infinite Banking Concept® or The Private Reserve Strategy™ may require that you stretch the parameters of your thinking a bit, or, as the popular saying goes, "think outside the box."

The kind of life insurance the concept uses is not the typical term life policy or traditional whole life policy, but a high cash value type of policy designed especially for this purpose. This kind of life insurance is probably the least understood of all the financial tools we have at our disposal. A historical dividend study from Mass Mutual displayed actual internal rates of returns between 1980 - 2008 of *4.5 - 6.5% per year average over the 28-year period.*

Terms are flexible. You can put as much or as little into your personal bank as you want. The growth is guaranteed and is not subject to market fluctuations. You have liquidity, use and control.

These accounts also have liquidity. The money is yours, after all. You should be able to use it any time you wish. In a traditional loan, you have to prove that you are able to pay the lending institution back. This involves credit checks and income verification. Since you are using your own money to collateralize the loan, none of that is required. A life insurance policy has no restrictions in that regard. It's as simple as telling the insurance company how much you want to borrow.

Recovering Opportunity Cost

Blanton makes the point that every dollar we do not save is consumed and lost forever. You may be able to replace it with future cash flow, but that money you spent is gone forever. That's not necessarily a bad thing; it's just the way things are. Take purchasing a car, for instance. Owning an automobile seems to have become a necessity in modern American life. Witness the fact that there are more than 250 million registered vehicles on the nation's roads. When you buy a car, you lose the amount of money you paid for that car. If you finance the car, you lose the interest you pay on the loan and if you pay cash you lose the amount of interest you could have earned had you been keep that money earning interest. I call that "opportunity cost."

If you look at car-buying long term, and in the light of how much it actually cost you over time, you may think twice. Let's say you bought a new car worth $30,000 and you financed that at 6% interest for 60 months. Your monthly payments would be $579.98 per month for a total of $34,799. You would have paid $4,799 in interest in the process. If you are just starting out in life, this will not be the only car you will ever own. For the rest of your adult life, you will probably own and drive a vehicle. Let's say that you have 40 more car-buying years left, and that every two years you trade cars and finance the purchase. That's 20 cars over the next 43 years. Assuming you could get 6% interest on money you saved, if you were able to only invest the interest you paid on those loans, you would have earned $463,203.

"What if I paid cash for the cars?"

Keep in mind, even if you paid cash, you still had an "opportunity" cost. "Either way, it works out to be the same," says Blanton.

Three Ways to Make Major Purchases

According to Blanton, there are three ways to make major, capital purchases like automobiles.

Going in debt. You may not have a choice. Millions of Americans don't, and that is what keeps the wheels of the banking industry turning. Debtors aren't earning any interest, so they are forced to pay interest.

Save up for it. Saving up for something in order to pay cash for it is an admirable discipline. Savers earn interest on their savings dollars and then pay for the purchase outright. Paying cash is better than borrowing money, but you still have to pay yourself back in some way or another. Then there's the third way:

Collateralize. This method is used by individuals who *could* pay cash for the purchase, but they understand that second principle of compound interest: it works best if left alone to grow. These are the ones who earn compound interest on their savings and they collateralize their major purchases. This is the method most conducive to creating wealth. Collateralization simply means to pledge a portion of one's money as security for an amortizing loan against one's cash purchases. That way, your money is still earning interest while you are paying interest.

An **amortized** loan, sometimes called an installment loan, is where monthly payments are applied first toward reducing the interest balance, and any remaining amount is applied toward the principal balance. As the loan is paid off, a progressively larger portion of the payments goes toward principal and a progressively smaller portion goes toward interest.

The Zero Line

To analyze this type of financial thinking, imagine a line going across the page we will call the zero line. It represents the financial position of someone who has nothing and owes nothing.

Going into debt. When someone has no money but still must make a purchase, they are forced to borrow against their future income. That forces them to go below zero to a certain point. Draw a straight line downward from the zero line to the debt amount. Now draw stair steps leading back to the zero line to represents the payments made by the debtor to get back to zero when the loan is paid off. If you are like most people in this category, now the process begins again. It's easy to get trapped in this endless cycle.

Saving up for it. Then there are those who save up for the item and pay cash. This method postpones gratification by essentially making "savings payments" above the zero line until they have accumulated enough to buy it with the cash. Draw stair steps representing those "savings payments" up from the zero line. Then the day comes to make the purchase. Now draw a straight line back to the zero line. That represents draining the tank to buy the item. The saver doesn't like being that close to the zero line, so they begin saving again until the next needed item must be purchased, and they drain the tank and the process starts again.

Collateralization. Those who create wealth have been saving just like the savers. But when it comes time to make a purchase, they borrow against their capital and pay off the lender while they continue to compound interest on their money. They made the same purchases as the other two, and they paid off their loans, just like the debtor and the saver, but the wealth creator earned the benefits of compound interest along the way. Draw a line continuing to climb, year by year, far above the zero line.

The Problem with Debt

Blanton describes debt as the act of borrowing money to buy things that you can't pay for in full with your monthly cash flow. A debtor is someone who has the intention to repay but does not have the ability to pay in full at the time of the purchase. The problem with debt is you have a future obligation against your earnings that you may or may not be able to fulfill. You not only lost the money you spent, but you had to pay interest to get it. When you go into debt, you essentially lose control of your cash flow. You have no control over the money you are spending to repay the debt. Repayment is forced upon you by terms of the agreement. Debt is not an efficient purchasing strategy.

The Problem with Paying Cash

Paying cash means you have to drain your savings – money that was earning, or had the potential to earn, compound interest. Depleting the savings means that you had to reset the compounding. The way compounding works puts me in mind of the old steam engine trains. They left the station slowly, chuffing great puffs of smoke and steam. They picked up speed slowly, but once they got moving, they moved faster and faster, using less energy to do it. When you reset compounding, you lose that initial momentum you worked so hard to build up. Think of the zero line again. For cash payers to truly get back to where they were before they drained the savings tank, they have to put back not only the amount they borrowed, but the interest they would have earned as well.

132

Another factor is taxes. In most accounts, any money earned is taxed either while it is in the account or upon withdrawal. Remember, compound interest works best over time and when it is not interrupted. Paying cash is not bad, but it's not the most efficient purchasing strategy.

The Future Effect of Paying Cash

Any time you drain the savings tank to pay for a substantial purchase with cash, you are resetting the compounding process. Paying cash keeps us from paying interest, true. But we still lose the interest we could be earning. Look at the long-term view. Say you have $50,000 in an account earning 5% compound interest. If you leave it alone, you will have $216,097 in 30 years. But let's say you had a major purchase you needed to make, so you drained the tank of the entire amount, but you put the money back within four years. The compounding momentum that you lost was costly indeed. The restored $50,000 account will only grow to $177,784 in the next 26 years. Big difference!

Why Not Be Your Own Bank?

One concept that successful wealth builders employ is to, in a sense, serve as their own lending institution. Wait a minute! Wouldn't that "rob the bank," so to speak? How would the banks make a profit if we were to stop paying interest to the bank and pay it to ourselves instead? That's just the point! This is a unique way to solve your need for capital while you are saving for your future. Here's how it works: Imagine a large piggy bank that represents an account with money in it. Call it "My Bank." Let's assume you want to make a major capital purchase, such as buying a car. Rather than draining your bank to do it, you secure a loan from a financial institution against the money you have in your bank. The lending institution gives you a check for the amount you want to borrow and you make your purchase. You now have an amortizing loan with the lending institution and they have a collateral position against your private bank. You will pay the institution declining interest while your private bank is earning compound interest. You are leveraging the difference between amortized payments and compounding interest only if the interest rate is higher. The most important thing is that you have liquidity, use and control of your cash and the compounding isn't interrupted.

To illustrate the difference between amortizing and compounding, let's say you have a $30,000 car loan on which you are paying 5% interest over a five-year period. Your monthly payments are $566. At the end of the five years, you would have paid $3,968 in interest. If you had $30,000 in an account earning 5% compound interest for those five years, you would have earned $8,501, while you were paying $3,968 in interest through the amortized car loan. However, you would have to use your future cash flow to pay down the car loan and that means you would lose the opportunity cost on those payments in the future.

What about mortgages? If you were to buy a house for $300,000 and pay cash, the cost over 30 years would be $1,340,323 in lost interest, assuming a 5% interest rate. If you finance $300,000 at the same 5% rate, the cost is going to be the same. The principle is the same even if the amounts you are dealing with are higher. Giving up your cash and the access to it is not the best alternative if you are able to leverage your own assets, earning compound interest while paying off an amortized loan.

Taxes and Cash Value Life Insurance

One of the few remaining legal and legitimate tax shelters left is cash value life insurance. There is a minimum one can pay for a given amount of insurance coverage for a specific age. Who determines that? The insurance company, naturally. They will tell you how much you must pay for indemnity on which they bear risk. Insurance companies and their actuaries calculate the least amount of premium they can charge and still make a profit. But is there a maximum you can put into a cash value life insurance policy? Yes. The government will tell you the maximum you can put into it. Why? Because of the tax advantages life insurance provides. Essentially the government has decided the upper limit of tax advantaged growth they will allow you to have. That tells me that it must be a good thing, if the government regulates it. If you buy more life insurance than the limit set by the government, it becomes what is called a Modified Endowment Contract (MEC) and is no longer tax advantaged.

Before the 1980s, there were no such restrictions in place. But the government essentially "drew the line" with two laws: the Technical and Miscellaneous Revenue Act of 1988 (TAMRA) and the Deficit Reduction Act of 1984 (DEFRA). Prior to TAMRA and DEFRA, people were able to put unlimited contributions in a life insurance policy and enjoy the tax benefits that went along with it. This was counter to the wishes of Uncle Sam that Americans sink their savings dollars into tax deferred accounts, such as 401(k)s, IRAs and SEPs.

Why would the government care? Because *deferred* taxes is a good thing for the tax collector. Taxes that are *deferred* are merely taxes *postponed.* Earlier in this book, I used the illustration of a farmer opting to pay tax on the seed instead of the harvest. The government knows what it is doing when it defers taxes. The IRS is in essence offering to let you pay tax on the harvest while giving you the seed tax free. They want your tax-deferred account to grow, just like a crop in the field, and when you when you withdraw the money you will be paying them more tax than you would have before. That's why the concept of Roth IRAs was such a welcome sight for tax savvy investors. With the Roth, you fund the account with dollars that have already been taxed and there is no more tax to be paid, ever!

Cash value life insurance is like a giant Roth in that respect. The money you put into the program has already been taxed but it grows tax-deferred and you can withdraw it tax-free.

Chapter Twenty

Making Every Dollar Count
in Retirement

For a state that receives 58 inches of rain every year, Florida, the state where I live, may seem to be impervious to drought. But 2006 - 2007 were the driest back-to-back calendar years Florida has experienced, based on data dating back to 1932. Weather records since 1900 reveals that in every decade there has been at least one severe and widespread drought somewhere in Florida.

During the 2006 - 2007 drought, we began paying attention to every drop that ran from our faucets. We didn't wash our cars or water our lawns and took shorter showers, and folks who had a social consciousness would even chastise those they saw wasting this precious resource. I remember thinking during one of those soap-up and rinse-off showers how much we take water for granted when there is a free flow of it and how much we waste when there is plenty to go around.

It's a little like that with our money. When we are working and there is a free flow of income, we don't hesitate to blow a few hundred here on a vacation or a few hundred there on some toy that catches our eye. But when we enter the retirement zone and we are living on the money we saved for that purpose, the income pipeline becomes very personal. We guard the outflow, realizing that the supply is finite and could be threatened by any number of financial predators.

That's why when you shift from living on the income and benefits available to you through your employment to living on a retirement income and benefits, you start seeing your money differently. I observe that most financial planning today seems designed primarily to help you *build* your retirement savings. But as you transition to and live in retirement, your needs and challenges can be very different. The goal of retirees, more often than not, shifts to properly managing money and making smart decisions that use resources more efficiently.

Retirement planning is personal. It is all about *you* and *your* family, not the average family or anyone else. You are unique. No one, regardless of how similar to yours their circumstances may be, is exactly like you. So when it comes to a plan for transitioning to and living in retirement, these individual differences make a huge difference. You are no longer in the saving and accumulating mode. You are now in the preservation and distribution mode. There may be issues relative to health care. Decisions made in retirement must be different from those made during your working years for many reasons. Medicare and Social Security move to the forefront. Should you work part-time in retirement? That depends on several factors. How will one income stream affect another? Do you have a few years left on a mortgage or have other debt? All of these factors make your situation unique. You need specialized retirement income planning. There are no cookie-cutter solutions that fit. Any recommendations from a professional simply must be built around your personal and unique situation. The key ingredient in all of this is to *make sure* that your money lasts as long as you do! Any financial plan that does not guarantee this is not a plan at all. It is a wish and a hope.

Build the Foundation First

When you are building a house, I sincerely doubt that you start on the roof first and then work down to the windows and the sashes. First, you build the foundation. Then comes the floor. Determining where you stand financially is usually the first order of business. Then comes the matter of ensuring that you have a lifetime safety net that is a "floor," so to speak – your basic needs – covered throughout retirement.

When I was taking the courses required to become a Retirement Management Analyst^{SM} (RMA^{SM}), I remember thinking how much sound financial planning is like constructing a well-made house. The first thing you do is establish the building budget. What are the sources of income available to you in retirement? If you are like most people, there may be several sources of income you need to manage. An RMA^{SM} will start by looking at your entire household and listing what you'll be getting from Social Security, any pensions you may be entitled to, plus any income you or your spouse are planning to get through part-time work or a business that you may own.

If you're just about to retire, knowing when to "turn on" your Social Security or pension income can make a big difference in the monthly amount that you get. A competent retirement management analyst will help you make those decisions, not emotionally, but mathematically.

How much you spend is a personal decision. But if you know where you stand and can make intelligent choices, you will be much better prepared for life in retirement. Your expenses will change dramatically when you make that change from working full time to a new retirement lifestyle. They may change again as the years of retirement roll by. For some, simplifying their lifestyle to reduce expenses may be in order. For others, they may wish to finally begin taking those trips they have been dreaming about for years. Or still others may have plans to start a new career or business, now that they have finished their "first career." Others may be planning to change locations. That may change the ball game considerably. Ordinary household expenses may change with the new location, and there are tax considerations to take into account. What about the overall cost of living and health care costs? When it comes to health care for those over 65, choosing the most appropriate plan available to them can be a daunting task without proper guidance. You will want to know how to get the most cost-effective Medicare benefits and how to best provide for what Medicare doesn't cover.

When you are doing your balance sheet prior to retirement and you realize your expenses add up to more than your income, what do you do? I call this the "moment of truth" in retirement planning. Something has to give, of course. You have to "right-size" your expenses to give you the proper amount of cash flow every month so you can continue to live a comfortable life. Once you've added up all your expenses, you may realize they add up to more than your income, so you start to figure out how you're going to right-size your expenses to give you the right amount of cash flow every month to live a comfortable life.

Discuss the Upside

Making every dollar count in retirement has to do with managing expenses, true. But one of the most vital pieces to the retirement planning puzzle is working with the retirement nest egg to make sure you make the most efficient use of those funds. Money needs to be put to work in retirement. Those dollars are like soldiers and they all need to be busy working in the most efficient manner possible, each doing their job of promoting your financial comfort once you are in the distribution phase of life. I call this "working with the upside." Some individuals may wish to leave a substantial legacy to their heirs. But that doesn't mean that you wrap the cash in plastic bags and bury it in a safe in the back yard. That "legacy money" needs to be put to work in a safe and efficient manner. A competent retirement management analyst can help you figure out how to create a "discretionary" fund within your investment assets to accomplish this.

The Retirement Financial Check-Up

Modern homes that are energy efficient make the energy used to heat and cool the structure go further. Insulation is thicker and windows are of double-wall construction so as not to waste one single British thermal unit (BTU) of energy. The cost savings of these "smart homes" is substantial. Folks who are thinking about retiring need to take the same approach with their financial houses. Could you benefit from a "check up?" Are there ways that your money could work harder and last longer? An RMA^{SM} has the specialized training to provide you with this type of planning, personalized to your unique situation and goals. If you are choosing a guide to take you on Safari, for example, you will more than likely want one who knows the jungle and is familiar with the lay of the land. Choosing a financial advisor who will help you create a secure retirement may be one of the most critical decisions you will ever make. Your advisor can play a pivotal role in ensuring your financial well-being and retirement income throughout many years in retirement. That's why it is so important to work with an advisor who has the specialized knowledge, education and ethical training related to effective retirement income planning and management. Professionals who have earned the RMA^{SM} certification have made the commitment to the advanced education that prepares them to help you achieve your goals and financial security in retirement. Advisors who hold the RMA^{SM} designation are also subject to continuing education requirements to make sure they stay on top of the latest research, products and trends in retirement income planning and management.

Outside the Box

Whatever your vision of retirement is, it is personal and uniquely yours. Some have visions of playing 36 holes of golf every sunny day and at least 18 when it's cloudy. Others want to finally relax and do nothing at all if nothing is what they choose to do. I know of one couple who has a two-year itinerary already established for touring the country with red pins marking the state and national parks they want to visit and blue pins representing their friends and relatives they plan to spend time with along the way. Some have grandchildren they will finally get to spend more time with. Then there are the world travelers who have the money saved up for traveling abroad.

In my line of work, I have observed the following is a fundamental truth: Money isn't necessarily the stuff of dreams, but it does help facilitate them. I love the line the late Zig Ziglar left us about money: "Money isn't the most important thing in life, but it's reasonably close to oxygen on the gotta have it scale."

I don't apologize if some of the concepts you have read in this book are novel and a step or two ahead of the march. Old investing ideas that no longer work must stand aside for the new ones that match our times. Those who hold to those failed concepts of the past are free to do so. But those who survive and thrive in their golden years during the 21st century will be those who learn to lean with the curves and think outside the box.

About the Author

Mark was born in New Jersey and grew up in the Fort Lauderdale area of Florida where his first job was working at a fast food restaurant. In school, Mark excelled in math. To this day he views helping clients manage and preserve their wealth as a numbers challenge – one which he thoroughly enjoys. Mark believes that there is no "silver bullet" when it comes to a successful, worry-free retirement. Rather, it is built one brick at a time by making intelligent choices. His planning philosophy is purpose-based, which is another way of saying that money means different things to different people and no two individuals are alike.

Mark believes that the most important financial aspect of retirement is a secure lifetime income.

Mark Lumia is Founder and CEO of True Wealth Group, LLC, which has its headquarters in Lady Lake, Florida in an area commonly known as "The Villages."

He and his wife, Maryna, make their home in Ocala, Florida. They are parents to two sons, Ian and Liam, and a daughter, Mia.

Mark started his career as a financial professional after leaving the University of Florida in 1989. He recognized that nothing gave him greater professional satisfaction than helping people preserve their wealth, retire with abundant income for the rest of their lives, and find ways to reduce their tax burdens. He formed True Wealth Group, LLC, and currently oversees a staff of four as Founder and CEO.

Mark is a Certified Financial Planner[®] (CFP[®]), Retirement Management Analyst[SM] (RMA[SM]) a Chartered Financial Consultant[®] (ChFC[®]) , and a Certified Advisor for Senior Living[®] (CASL[®]). He holds numerous other licenses and credentials such as Series 6, 7, 24, 26, 63 and 65. He is a Master Elite IRA Advisor[®] and an Infinite Banking Concepts[®] Authorized Practitioner. He also holds a Real Estate License. While Mark specializes in retirement income planning, his office also helps clients with Medicare and Social Security planning.

The author appreciates your comments about the material in this book. Please send your remarks to Mark@TrueWealthGroup.com.

You may contact Mark R. Lumia at

True Wealth Group, LLC
13940 N. US Highway 441, Suite 601
Lady Lake, Florida 32159
1-800-7Mark72 or 1-800-762-7572